D1298539

SURVIVAL
IN SARAJEVO

Die Deutsche Bibliothek – CIP-Einheitsaufnahme

Serotta, Edward:
Survival in Sarajevo: how a Jewish Community came to Aid
of its City / Edward Serotta. – Vienna: Brandstätter, 1994
Dt. Ausg. u. d. T.: Serotta, Edward: Überleben in Sarajewo
ISBN 3-85447-572-I

This publication is issued in conjunction with the exhibition *Survival in Sarajevo*

In North America an exhibition from the Jewish Museum of Vienna and the Judah M Magnes Museum

Saidye Bronfman Centre for the Arts
Montreal
February–March 1995

The Spertus Museum of Art Chicago
April–August 1995

Duke University Chapel Hill
Autumn 1995

The Judah M Magnes Museum
Berkeley
Winter 1996

In Europe an exhibition from the Jewish Museum of Vienna

Jewish Museum Vienna
September–November 1994

Austrian Cultural Center Prague
November–December 1994

City Museum Munich
December 1994–January 1995

Jewish Museum Hohenems
February–March 1995

Alte Synagoge Essen
April–May 1995

Museo Sefardi de Toledo
September–October 1995

Municipality of Rome
January 1996

In Europe an exhibition curated by the Jewish Historical Museum Amsterdam

Jewish Historical Museum
Amsterdam
November 1994–January 1995

Palais Jalta Frankfurt
February–March 1995

Bosna Gallery Sarajevo
Summer 1995

Exhibitions of Survival in Sarajevo *are in the permanent collections of*
Beth Hatefutsoth Museum of the Diaspora Tel Aviv (June–September 1994)

and Jewish Museum Berlin (April–May 1995)

First published in Austria in 1994 by Christian Brandstätter Verlag, A-1080 Wien, Wickenburggasse 26
and
Central Europe Center for Research & Documentation, D-10715 Berlin, Bruchsaler Straße 7.

Distributed in the United States by
D. A. P. (Distributed Art Publishers), 636 Broadway, 12th Floor, New York, N. Y. 10012
Tel.: (212) 473-5119, Fax: (212) 673-2887

Copyright © 1994 by Christian Brandstätter Verlag, Wien
Text copyright © 1994 Edward Serotta
Photographs copyright © 1994 Edward Serotta
All rights reserved. No part of this publication may be reproduced, stored in a retrieval system, or transmitted,
in any form or by any means, electronic, mechanical, photocopying, recording, or otherwise,
without the prior written permission of the publisher.
ISBN 3-85447-572-1

Editor: Deborah Wise
Designers: Christian Brandstätter and Edward Serotta
Production: Franz Hanns
Printed and bound in Austria by Druckhaus Grasl, Bad Vöslau

EDWARD SEROTTA

SURVIVAL IN SARAJEVO

How a Jewish Community Came to the Aid of its City

Edition Christian Brandstätter · Wien

For Denis

Table of contents

The final battle of the Second World War on Yugoslav soil took place in Slovenia in May 1945. Communist *Partizans* surrounded German and Croatian fascists. Among the *Partizans* were Moris Albahari, 15, and Djuro Fischer, 17. Both boys were Jewish. Moris was from Sarajevo. Djuro, from Novi Sad, was the only member of his family to escape deportation.

The two boys had been together for three years, running messages for generals, attending *Partizan* schools on the run, sometimes fighting. Djuro was present on a snowy, winter morning in a stable in the Bosnian mountains when a handful of Jewish doctors, reciting prayers from memory, helped Moris with his Bar Mitzvah. Djuro and Moris were best friends, inseparable.

During this final battle, a grenade fell into the boys' trench and blew off Djuro's legs at his thighs. As he lay dying in Moris's arms, he asked his friend to say Kaddish for him, the Jewish prayer for the dead. It took the boy twenty minutes to die. Moris held him, prayed, and sobbed. The battle raged on. Moris stayed with the body of his friend through the night. The next morning, he turned back toward Sarajevo and began walking. Twenty-eight days later he reached the city.

"Everything that was Jewish had been wrecked, ruined, or burned," he said. "The synagogues were destroyed, everyone's homes had been looted by the Germans or Fascists, then turned over to refugees. Of all my friends, only two, Binko and Rafaelo, survived. They had hidden in Italy and soon they left for Israel. My parents were alive, but of the 64 other members of our family, my cousins and aunts and uncles and grandparents, not one was left. These first months of families returning were surely the hardest and saddest for all of us."

Nearly 12,000 Jews lived in Sarajevo in March, 1941. They made up 13 % of its population; 8,000 were *Sephardim* who traced their roots directly to the expulsion from Spain in 1492. They may have kept mostly to themselves and spoke in *Ladino*, based on a 15th century Spanish dialect and written with Hebrew characters, but over the centuries they became part of the fabric of Sarajevo. They never lived in a ghetto, there had never been a pogrom against them, and they were not restricted to certain trades. In the municipal ballot of 1928, five of the 35 city council members elected were Jews.

The Sarajevo Moris Albahari returned to in 1945 had lost 8,000 Jews in the Holocaust. The colorful world they had inhabited, and that had enriched their city, was no more. A mere 1,400 Jews registered at the Jewish community center that year. An aid bureau opened in the one synagogue that remained. Workers from Joint (the American Jewish Joint Distribution Committee), which had been helping and rescuing Jews in Europe and the Middle East since 1914, set up a food and clothing center. They provided cash donations, medical care, and housing allowances. Field reports written by Joint workers then, typed on onion skin paper now resting in archives in New York, speak of the determination and dedication of the city's Jews, of their willingness to rebuild and re-organize. Little wonder when one considers who survived.

Throughout Yugoslavia, a large percentage of the Jews who survived did so by fighting. This was unique in Nazi-occupied Europe. The majority of those who survived in other lands were not given the chance to join a guerrilla army and spent the war in exile, ghettos, or concentration camps. Nearly a thousand Sarajevo Jews joined the *Partizans*. They fought with Tito and a third of them died in combat. After the war 46 were decorated for bravery and four were given National Hero citations, the equivalent of the US Congressional Medal of Honor. Hundreds of other Sarajevo Jews survived in hiding, protected by friends, neighbors, and, for those who made it across the Adriatic, the Italians.

Danilo Nikolich was three years old when his father escaped the Nazis to join the *Partizans*. His mother Donka, watching the round-up of the Jews, grabbed her son and fled into the hills. They spent the entire war going from village to village and were fed, housed, and hidden by Serbs, Muslims, and Croats. Danilo would never forget this.

Jacob Finci was born while his parents were in hiding in Italy. After the war they were invited to stay. "But while my parents were more grateful than you can imagine, they could not bear the thought of being refugees from Sarajevo. So our family returned home to Bosnia."

In Sarajevo, there had been collaborators, informers, even a brigade of Muslim fascists during the war. But there were also men like Mustafa Hardaga, a Muslim who told his wife Zeyneba, "you do not abandon your friends." The Hardaga family hid their Jewish friend Josef Kabilio from the Nazis, and after helping him escape to safety, Zeyneba's father hid and protected another Jewish man. He was informed on by a Nazi collaborator, arrested, and shipped off to his death in a concentration camp.

There may have been only 6,500 Jews in the whole of Yugoslavia during the communist period, but they built one of the liveliest, most hard working, and welcoming communities in Europe. That they were no longer rich nor powerful did not seem to faze them. Religious practice was infrequent. Most had intermarried. But their bustling, noisy community centers were filled with children, teenagers, families, and the elderly. They published books, magazines, newspapers, calendars, and literary quarterlies. They were proud of their kindergartens, museums, libraries, the old-age home and summer camp, Hebrew classes, theater productions. They brought food to the elderly, visited the

Jacob Finci at the Jewish community's two-way radio. December 1994.

sick, and tended the cemeteries. They taught their children to remember and memorialize the past while at the same time to build and learn for the future. Despite the paucity of their numbers, this was no dying, "*last Jews*" community.

Their partner in all this, again, was Joint. Along with the Central British Fund for World Jewish Relief, the Memorial Foundation for Jewish Culture in New York, and the Doron Foundation of Tel Aviv, a steady supply of funds, packaged youth programs, and scholarships was channeled to Yugoslav Jewry along with the people who helped implement them. By the 1980s, $ 1.4 million had been invested.

By the end of that decade the old *Partizan* fighters who rebuilt Jewish life in Bosnia had all retired and a new guard had taken over the community. Danilo Nikolich, who was an engineer, and Jacob Finci, now a corporate lawyer, were appointed to the community's board of directors. Ivan Ceresnjes, who was not even from Sarajevo, became the first non-Sephardi to head the community as president. His mother was from Croatia, his father, Alexander, a Hungarian.

Ivan only came face to face with his father a handful of times, but Alexander Ceresnjes was the stuff of legends for his son. Here was a man who joined the first short-lived communist government of Hungary in 1919. He fought against the Fascists in Spain, the Nazis in North Africa and Italy, and at war's end returned to Budapest and worked in the foreign ministry. Arrested and tried in a show trial, he was tortured and imprisoned for a decade and died a broken man. Growing up in Sarajevo, Ivan kept and treasured every article written about his father. A successful architect, married with three children, Ivan never thought he would ever have the chance to be as brave, as courageous, or as foolhardy in the face of danger as his father had been. But he was wrong.

By 1991, Yugoslavia was collapsing. Nikolich, Finci and Ceresnjes met to discuss the future. Slovenia and Croatia were about to secede. What would that mean for Bosnia? For the Jews of Sarajevo?

It was in March 1992, well after Slovenia had successfully seceded from Yugoslavia, and Croatia had wrenched itself away with considerably less success and more bloodshed, that war came to Bosnia. A month later Sarajevo was besieged by the Bosnian Serbs and cut off from the world. The shelling would last 22 months, the siege even longer.

Others have written about the military situation and political crises in Bosnia. Photo-journalists have recorded the destruction of the city. These were not my tasks. I went to Sarajevo because for the first time during a modern European war, Jews have been actively saving and rescuing Christians and Muslims wherever, whenever they could. Because I have been working in Central Europe for nearly a decade, almost exclusively as a chronicler of contemporary Jewish life, I felt compelled to be there and document this story.

Danilo Nikolich in his office in the Sarajevo Jewish community. February 1994.

For many people, since 1948, heroism and Jews equaled one thing: Israel. The battle for Independence, the creation of a nation-state in the desert, the ensuing wars against overwhelming odds. Events like these defined Jewish heroism in our time. By contrast, Diaspora Jewish communities, in the Americas and Western Europe especially, have integrated comfortably into their respective societies. But suddenly in Sarajevo, a remnant Jewish community has turned contemporary history on its head. Middle age, middle class, professional men and women have been carrying out heroic deeds, assisted by friends and neighbors of every age and nationality.

In this ethnic conflict between Serbs, Croats, and Muslims, the Jews of Bosnia play no contentious part. The warring factions respect that and seem to have issued an undeclared 'hands-off' policy. That means the Jews were not forced to choose sides. Many have refused to condemn one faction or the other, while remaining fiercely loyal to the city they

have lived in and loved for four hundred and thirty years.

Outside Sarajevo, there are those who speak of the Croatian *Ustasha* fascists who murdered Jews wholesale during the Second World War. Others offer evidence that show Serbia's quisling General Nedic turned some Jews over the Nazis (although nothing the Serbs did could compare to the bestiality of the *Ustasha*). Still others remind the world of the Muslim SS brigade, the Handjar. But in Sarajevo, elderly Jewish men and women claim that their lives were saved during the Holocaust by Croats, Serbs, and Muslims. They refuse to issue a verdict of collective guilt. They say they were saved by individual acts of bravery.

The majority of Sarajevo's Jews fled the city in the early months of this war to Israel, England, and elsewhere. But a vital core remained and decided they would open the doors of their synagogue to everyone. They re-launched their own humanitarian aid society, La Benevolencija, which had been dormant since 1941. With an infrastructure and warehouse run in cooperation with Joint in the Croatian port city of Split, inside the besieged Bosnian capital they were joined by Serbs, Croats, Muslims, and Jews: doctors, cooks, dentists, policemen, journalists, teachers, children, college students, housewives, pensioners, and elderly *Partizan* fighters. Not one of whom had done a day's social work in their lives.

These 54 volunteers went to work each day in a faded pink synagogue as Sarajevans became dependent on the humanitarian aid brought to them by the Red Cross, the International Rescue Committee, the Soros Foundation, UNHCR, Médecins Sans Frontières, Merkhamet, Catholic Aid and other organizations (helped in no small part by brave and determined local citizens).

During the siege, from May 1992 to February 1994, La Benevolencija opened three pharmacies, gave away 1,600,000 medical prescriptions, cooked 110,000 hot meals in an impromptu kitchen, and distributed 360 tons of food in the synagogue's social hall. Their three doctors and three nurses saw 2,500 patients in a jerry-rigged medical clinic and made 650 house calls. With no international mail operating, La Benevolencija started its own post office and brought 100,000 letters in and out of Sarajevo. Joint sent in a two way radio and linked it to a Zagreb office. It made 9,500 connections to the outside world and received 10,000 personal messages. Teachers gave foreign language lessons in the community lounge and Clowns performed for children. A weekend-long festival of Sephardic culture was arranged for the 500th anniversary of the expulsion of Jews from Spain.

Ivan Ceresnjes in the community center lounge. January 1994.

La Benevolencija, in conjunction with friends and colleagues abroad, also sent eleven convoys out of the city, three by air, eight by bus. This brought 2,300 Sarajevans to safety, among whom less than half were Jews. The Jewish Agency for Israel arranged for nearly 650 Bosnians to go to Israel and in so doing, stretched the "Who Is A Jew" law to new and creative limits.

Why did Sarajevo's Jews want to help at all? What is it about these people that prepared them, as if by instinct, for trouble while most Sarajevans did not believe the worst would ever happen? How could it be that the Jewish community center had stocks of food, medicine and clothing well before the first shell was fired?

The answer, of course, lies in history. The men and women who ran the community during the siege of Sarajevo knew a painful past, intertwined with war, revolution, Holocaust, and renewal. Some Sarajevo Jews still keep the house keys their refugee ancestors brought from Spain. A collective memory runs deep in Jews.

The most fitting tribute I found came not from Sarajevans today but from Ivo Andric, a Bosnian writer who won the Nobel Prize for Literature in 1961. In his novel **Bosnian Chronicle**, set in the first two decades of the 1800s, the French Consul is about to leave Travnik, seat of the Turkish Viziers ruling Bosnia. Back in France, Napoleon's regime had fallen and the Consul was without funds. He did not want to ask for help, even though the Vizier had bragged how he had recently forced Travnik's Jews to turn over all their cash.

It was Solomon Atijas, an elderly Jew, who offered funds as Jews everywhere held France in high regard after Napoleon emancipated them throughout his empire. Flabbergasted at the generosity, the Consul asked how it was Travnik's Jews had anything left to give. Atijas replied:

"The Vizier is a hard man, truly hard and difficult. Viziers come and go ... and each of them takes something with him, that's true ... but we Jews remain, we remember, we keep a tally of all we've been through, of how we have defended and preserved ourselves, and we pass on these dearly bought experiences from father to son. And so our cash boxes have two bottoms. One is just deep enough for the Vizier to reach down and scoop clean, but underneath a little something always remains for us and our children, for the salvation of our soul, for helping ourselves and our friends when they're in need."

During the siege of the city, Sarajevo's Jews had precious little cash lying around. But they did have friends abroad who helped, and with their support, they threw themselves into the task of teaching their fellow Sarajevans the lesson Jews have been learning for centuries: how to survive.

This is their story.

[1]   *Jewish Community of Sarajevo*, Dr Mario Levi, published by the Jewish Community of Sarajevo, 1984.

Keys from Spain

Where is the key that was in the drawer
My forefathers brought it here with great love
They told their sons, this is the heart
Of our home in Spain
Dreams of Spain
Traditional Sephardic Song

All during that last week of January, snow clouds drifted over the mountains of central Bosnia and gently let loose their load over towns and villages. In the capital Sarajevo, red tiled roofs disappeared under sheets of white; old Turkish houses surrounding courtyards were hung with icicles. It bore all the earmarks of a cozy winter scene, only this was 1994 and many roofs had been torn apart by mortar shells, historic buildings were burnt out hulks, and this January 18 children were killed by mortars fired from the hills overlooking the city.

The old Turkish quarter of Mostar. Jews were welcomed to southeastern Europe by the ruling Ottoman Turks. July 1988.

The day the snow let up, Jacob Finci, president of La Benevolencija, found me drinking coffee in the community center's lounge. He asked if I wanted to take a walk. "I have something to show you," he said.

There had been little shelling that morning and we strolled through the old Turkish quarter and up the hill, past a mosque whose garden was filled with war-time graves, and a skeleton of an apartment house. We headed for the city museum before us, a grandiose terra cotta edifice built by the Turks in the middle 1800s.

Jacob rang the bell and the director, dressed in several sweaters and a pair of worn house shoes, swung open the massive wooden door. He led us through elegant courtyards where gardens and fountains sat buried under snow, and through bare exhibition rooms. Everything was in storage during the siege, he said apologetically. His voice and our footsteps echoed as we went. We entered his cozy book-lined office, which now had a bed in it for him and his wife.

The director carefully drew three heavy keys from a woolen cloth and laid them on a table near the window. Jacob said, "When the Jews were expelled from Spain in 1492, many took their house keys and the keys to their synagogues with them. They always hoped they would return. They always dreamed this dream. But of course, they did not go back and in time these keys ended up here in Sarajevo." He chuckled. "Along with us."

The word *Sepharad* means Spain in Hebrew and dates back to the period Jews first came to Iberia after the destruction of the Second Temple in Jerusalem in 79 AD. It was in the 10th and 11th centuries, as Islamic power reached its zenith in Spain, that Jewish life flourished alongside it. This was a period of such rich cultural output that it is considered one of the golden ages of the Jewish people. In Córdoba, Seville, and Granada, Jews created some of the finest religious and secular poetry ever written in the Hebrew language. They made their first great discoveries in medicine and pharmacology. Jewish philosophy was suffused with ideas from Islam and strongly influenced by the greatest Jewish thinker of the age, Moses Maimonides. Jews were accepted in the Islamic courts as physicians, diplomats, and financiers, and were often called

The Jewish cemetery of Sarajevo dates from the 1600s. August 1988.

upon as arbitrators in disputes between Christians and Muslims.

This period ended in 1147 when the Almohads, a fanatical Berber dynasty, swept into Spain from Morocco. Many Jews fled north into Christian Spain, where for over a century they were welcomed and protected. As southern territory was re-conquered from the Muslims, Jews were offered land grants and tax incentives to resettle there. Politically neutral, they posed no threat to their rulers and many worked with their princes to rebuild commerce and industry and aided in the transition from Muslim to Christian rule.[1]

The climate began to change in the middle of the 13th century. Church leaders in Barcelona sought to limit the influence of the Jews by prohibiting them from public office. The first blood libel trial was held in Sargossa in 1250. In 1391, anti-Jewish riots broke out in Castile. Andalusia and Valencia followed suit.

Hundreds of Jews were murdered and throughout the land, the Church forced Jews to convert to Christianity (the *Conversos*) or face execution by burning. Jews were herded into ghettos in Castile and religious zealots confiscated copies of the Talmud in several cities.

In 1469, Ferdinand, heir to the crown of Aragon, married Isabella, heiress to the Castilian crown, and ten years later their kingdoms merged. This spelled doom for Spanish Jewry. The Inquisition began in 1480; tens of thousands of Jews and *conversos* were tortured, thousands more were burned to death. Andalusia expelled all Jews in 1483.

The armies of Ferdinand and Isabella finally routed the Muslims from Granada, their last European stronghold, in December 1491. Now all of Spain was united under Catholic rule. Three months later, the expulsion order was issued to the Jews.[2] Fifteen centuries of Spanish Jewish culture came to an

The white leather driving gloves and photograph of Julius Brod, a Czech Jew who settled in Bosnia after the Austrian occupation in 1878. Brod, the first engineer of The Royal and Imperial Austrian Railroad, drove Archduke Franz Ferdinand to Sarajevo in 1914, where he was assassinated.

abrupt end. Stunned and shocked, the Jews had but weeks to sell their possessions, their homes, their treasured libraries, businesses, and vineyards.

Cast out from the land they loved, they could not – nor would they ever – come to terms with the enormity of this loss. From that date on, their songs and poems were filled with pain and longing, sadness and nostalgia. They left almost everything behind and they left in tears. But they brought with them their keys and dreams that they might one day return. I held three of those keys that cold winter day in 1994.

In 1565 the first *Sephardim* reached the Miljacka river valley in central Bosnia and the village that lay below called Sarajevo. Two generations removed from their cherished land, they brought with them their language and customs, their store of knowledge and love of learning. But the Sephardim would never again attain the heights they had reached in

Spain. They had come from a glittering, rich world to one so far removed that they did not consider it Europe.

The Bosnia they settled into was a harsh land and a poor one, ruled severely by the Ottoman Turks since 1463. Downtrodden peasants eked out existence in villages caked with mud in winter, dust in summer. However, unlike most European rulers, the Ottoman sultans invited these landless Jews to settle and live in their midst.

The Sephardim kept to themselves, maintained their traditions, but became an integral part of Bosnian society because they possessed badly needed skills. They excelled in metal crafts and leather tanning. They traded in glass, textiles, and furs. Centuries of study taught them pharmacology and medicine. In Sarajevo, Jewish pharmacists sat in their stalls offering cures and homeopathic remedies. Nutmeg was good for breathing problems, camo-

17

mile was for stomach cramps. Spanish fly was recommended for dog bites – and love affairs.[3]

As the Turkish Empire grew and expanded in the 17th and 18th centuries, so did the fortunes of Sarajevo, which became one of its major trading cities. Jews operated the first sawmill and printing press in Bosnia and expanded their trade to iron, wood, and chemicals. According to the Encyclopedia Judaica, by the 1800s nearly all doctors in Bosnia were Jewish.

However, the majority of Jews remained poor. They had large extended families and several generations lived together in a single room. As *rayahs* (non-Muslims) they and Christians were subject to special laws. They were not allowed to wear green, for example, and paid higher taxes. Jews were also supposed to act as laborers on roads and bridges, but in practice, the Jewish community leadership made payments to city authorities that relieved them of such chores.[4]

Site where Serb nationalist Gavrilo Princip shot Austrian Archduke Franz Ferdinand in 1914. May 1989.

Their first synagogue, *Il Kal Grande*, dated from the mid-1580s and was surrounded by a courtyard and house for the poor. Several fires destroyed the original structure but the walls of the synagogue, built of the soft mellow stones that also line its courtyard, still remain. Even now, on hot dusty days, not infrequent in the Balkans, tall shade trees filter out the glaring sunlight overhead and create a languid and evocative shrine to this lost Sephardic world.

The cemetery these Sephardim built is no less enchanting. In the mid-1600s, Rabbi Samuel Baruch sold the Jewish community a plot of land on a hillside in Kovacici above the town. His grave, still preserved, dates from 1661. All the gravestones weigh between one-and-a-half to four tons and were hewn from white stone in a nearby quarry. For centuries, these oblong, rounded shapes, called "sleeping lions" , have peered out over the city from their hilly perch. Little is known of their history. There are no others like them anywhere in the world.

Jews in this part of the Ottoman Empire were on relatively good terms with their neighbors, but like everyone else, they were subject to the whims and tantrums of the viziers and pashas who ruled them. In the beginning of the 1800s, the newly arrived Ruzdi Pasha demanded the Jews pay a penalty of five hundred gold coins to compensate for supposed misdeeds of one of their own. When the Pasha took a handful of Jews and Christians hostage, 3,000 Muslims rose in protest to liberate them. The Pasha fled, dispatching a hasty letter to Istanbul demanding justice from the Sultan against the Jews. But before his letter arrived, the Sarajevo Jews sent their own petition, and the Sultan issued a decree for the Pasha's immediate dethronement.[5]

According to Jane Gerber in "The Jews of Spain: A History of the Sephardic Experience," the Sephardim were a restless lot, intellectually and spiritually. Over the centuries they sought reasons and explanations for the expulsion from their beloved homeland. Some rabbis turned on their Spanish predecessors who had flirted with rationalism and Arabic philosophy. Others immersed themselves in messiasnism, kabbalism, and numerology. According to 17th century Jewish numerologists, 1648 would see the return of the Messiah, preceded by terrible events. In that year, pogroms in Poland and the emergence of Sabbetai Zevi as spiritual leader appeared to bear out the prophecy.

Born in the Turkish city of Izmir, Zevi was deeply involved in messianism. His preachings overturned traditional Jewish law and he gathered a following that quickly grew in number and intensity. In 1665 Zevi declared himself the Messiah and word spread throughout the Empire. Muslim authorities arrested him in 1666. When the Sultan gave Zevi the choice of death or conversion to Islam, he quickly chose the latter, leaving his followers stunned.

While the aftershocks of this false messiah spread throughout the entire Jewish world, its effect on Ottoman Jewry was enormous, catastrophic. Spiritually shaken, Jewish communities throughout the Empire experienced a profound sense of depression from which some never recovered.

When Ottoman rule began collapsing in 1878 and Bosnia was occupied by the Austrians, the first large migration of German and Yiddish speaking Jews arrived in Sarajevo. The differences between these Ashkenazim and the Sephardim were immediately apparent. The German speaking Jews (or *Svabo Jijos* as the Sephardim derisively dubbed them) were outgoing, well educated in public schools, solidly middle class, and versed in the ways of a Europe undergoing a decisive change of industrial activity and intellectual ferment. The majority of the Sephardim, on the other hand, were insular, poorly educated, and aside from a few wealthy Sephardi industrialists, worked as artisans and unskilled laborers. Jewish community record books showed that their names swelled the lists of those who could not afford to pay taxes. The two communities had very little to do with each other and the Ashkenazim built their own synagogue on the banks of the Miljacka River.

Site where Serb nationalist Gavrilo Princip shot Austrian Archduke Franz Ferdinand in 1914. November 1993.

The Austrians brought capitalism to Sarajevo. Their investments in infrastructure and industry geared Bosnia's production and trade toward the needs of their Empire to the north: Vienna, Prague, Budapest and Trieste. The Sephardim, whose connections were primarily with the coastal cities of Split, Venice, and Ragusa (Dubrovnik), went rapidly into economic decline.

The Sephardi community created La Benevolencija in 1892 to help. At first this charitable organization, funded by wealthy Sephardim, provided medical assistance and financial aid. By the turn of the century it had expanded its activities toward education. Hundreds of students went to high school and university on La Benevolencija scholarships. Its programs were opened to the Ashkenazim in the 1920s. La Benevolencija supported cultural programs, lecture series, job counseling, adult educa-tion courses, and underwrote serious publishing efforts. It also occasionally aided Croatian, Serb, and Muslim humanitarian organizations.[6] Due to the dedication of its directors, Sephardic Jewry in Sarajevo was given a new lease on intellectual life. Within two decades of its founding, Sephardi women were becoming writers and poets, children of semi-literates were earning doctoral degrees, and the first Rabbinical seminary opened in Sarajevo.

In 1908 Bosnia was annexed into the Austro-Hungarian Empire. This brought about a dramatic rise in tension between Serbia and Austria. While visiting Sarajevo on 28 June, 1914, the anniversary of the Serb defeat by the Turks in 1389, Austrian Archduke Franz Ferdinand was assassinated by Gavrilo Princip, a young Serb nationalist.

The four years of war that followed swept away all the continent's great dynasties. For the first time in centuries, the hodge-podge of peoples ruled by Austria-Hungary and Turkey were left to forge their own states, each marked by heatedly disputed borders. The Kingdom of Serbs, Croats and Slovenes (soon to be known as Yugoslavia) came together in an uneasy union. During its two decades of life prior to the Second World War, Serb hegemony clashed angrily with Croatian and Slovenian demands for greater autonomy. Even if Hitler's forces had not overrun Yugoslavia in 1941, many historians believed this interwar state was destined to tear itself apart.

1   *The Jews of Spain: A History of the Sephardic Experience.* Jane S. Gerber. pps 92–95.
2   *The Jews of Spain: A History of the Sephardic Experience.* Jane S. Gerber. pps 116–138.
3   *Die Sephardim in Bosnien: Ein Beitrag zur Geschichte der Juden auf der Balkanhalbinsel.* Moritz Levy. 1911.
4   Harriet Pass Friedenreich, *The Jews of Yugoslavia: A Search for Identity.* pps 14–15.
5   Levy, a Jew from Sarajevo, wrote this study, based on community, city and Turkish records for his doctoral thesis and went on to become a rabbi in the city. He was deported to his death during the Second World War.
6   Harriet Pass Friedenreich, *The Jews of Yugoslavia: A Search for Identity.* pps 117–118.

The Shadow of War, I

Captured on film near the turn of the 20th century, put behind glass and framed on a wall, Jews in lavish Sephardic dress still peer out at those who come for lunch in the Sarajevo Jewish community center. I had noticed these time-worn photographs on my first visit in 1988 and they were still there five years later. There were also a few old souls who came to the community every day who could recall a world of bearded men in flowing caftans and bejeweled women serving sweets from Turkish divans. But before these people reached adulthood, that traditional world was brutally destroyed. A half century after the destruction, during the winter's siege in 1993, I watched them enter the lounge from the street, shaking off snow from their overcoats and ice from their boots. They smoked their strong Drina cigarettes and, if there was any, drank a cup of coffee. They sat together over lunch, then presented an empty pot to Tzitzko, the cook, which he filled for their dinner, and these elderly Jews headed cautiously home again, the last witnesses to one lost world, living now in another lost world.

In time I began intruding, asking them questions about their past lives, and the milieu they had grown up in and saw destroyed. Some spoke with me for hours. Often they spoke about war, interrupted occasionally by the shriek of a mortar shell overhead.

Life changed dramatically in 1940, when, as a sop to the Nazis, Yugoslavia passed its first Numerus Clausus laws that restricted Jewish enrollment in schools and universities. Panic spread, but the Jewish communities went into action immediately and took in their own students along with out-of-work Jewish teachers to help them. They set up high schools and vocational schools and when jobs were denied Jews, they created classes for re-training workers and opened soup kitchens.

On 25 March 1941, representatives of the Royal Yugoslav government signed a non-aggression pact with the Nazis in Vienna. Twenty four hours later they were overthrown in Belgrade. On 6 April the country was invaded by the Germans and their allies. Capitulation came on 17 April.

Adolf Hitler carved up the state and threw its pieces to those who craved to devour it: Bulgaria, Hungary, Romania, Italy and Albania. None of the six countries that administered Yugoslavia, save the Italians, spared its Jews.[1] One letter received by a Joint worker in the Summer of 1941 from a man named Klein in Zagreb detailed the horrors facing the city's 12,000-strong Jewish community. Families were collected and sent to live in open-air compounds. Everything in their homes was confiscated. Furniture went to the Ustasha, bed sheets to hospitals, and the rest was carted away into storage. Families were separated and men sent to work in salt mines. There was precious little food. In the evenings, Jews were selected for deportation, then sent away in the middle of the night in sealed cattle cars. "We no longer live from day to day, but from hour to hour," wrote Mr Klein. Zagreb was cleared of Jews.

Soon after the Axis-led partition of Yugoslavia, several guerrilla bands formed to fight the invaders. The Communists, led by Tito (born Josip Broz, a Slovene/Croat), started highly disciplined fighting units called the Partizans. Draza Mihailovich, a colonel in the Royal Yugoslav Army, led a mostly Serb band who called themselves Chetniks, named for the legendary Serb fighters. The Ustasha and the German Army fought them both, while the Chetniks and Partizans just as often took on each other.

Only the Partizans by and large welcomed Jews. Slavko Goldstein, in *The Jews of Yugoslavia*, estimated between 4,000–5,000 Jews joined the Partizans and one of Tito's closest advisers, Moshe Pijade, was a Jew.

Elias Danon in his Sarajevo apartment. December 1993.

The German Army entered Sarajevo on 16 April, 1941 and immediately sacked all eight synagogues. Treasures that were not stolen were burned. Centuries of record books, precious silver, ancient libraries, and illuminated manuscripts – nearly the sum total of Sarajevo's Jewish heritage – was carted off or went up in smoke.

An apparently knowledgeable German officer raced to the National Museum for one of Bosnia's great prizes: the Sarajevo Hagaddah, a 14th century illuminated manuscript from Spain called by scholars one of the most important Jewish books in the world The director, Jozo Petrovich, calmly explained that it had just been given to another German officer. In reality, one of the museum's Arab scholars, Dervis Korkut, was just then spiriting the book

away under his arm, through the city and up to the mountain of Bjelasnica, where a peasant kept it safe until the end of the war.[2]

Those Sarajevo Jews who did not flee or join the Partizans were rounded up and shoved into buildings where they awaited deportation. Most were herded onto trains in the Autumn of 1941 and sent to the Ustasha run concentration camp in Jasenovac.[3]

Three separate camps were built on its grounds, two of which had factories and kilns that provided the Croatian Army with supplies. It took little time for the internees – Serbs, Jews, Gypsies, and political enemies alike – crowded into unheated wooden barracks and fed next to nothing, to succumb to the inhuman conditions. Medicines given to the camp's Croatian commanders by relief agencies were found piled in garbage dumps. The few Jews who managed to survive Jasenovac were sent to Auschwitz while those women and children who had been left behind in Sarajevo were deported between December 1941 and January 1942.

By the following summer, there was no evidence of Jewish life in Sarajevo. Homes and businesses had been looted or occupied, synagogues stood ruined, and the Jewish cemetery on the hill, with no one to care for it, was covered over with weeds and high grass. Three hundred and seventy five years of Bosnian Jewry had come to a muted, tragic end.

One of the survivors of that destroyed world was Moris Albahari. Albahari, a Sephard, can trace both sides of his family back to the expulsion from Spain. His grandfather was a saraf, Turkish for money-changer. His mother's side of the family were kosher butchers and ritual slaughterers for Jewish communities in smaller outlying towns such as Kladanj.

Albarahi's father was one of six brothers. They owned five hardware and clothing stores, three in Sarajevo and two in Banja Luka, where Moris was born in 1930. In that year the family moved to Sarajevo. Moris and his three sisters grew up in a world of Sephardic traditions and customs.

"Ladino was spoken in homes and on the street, and the Sephardic Jews kept much to themselves, something like the Turks," he said. "Most dressed in the modern way even then, but you could still see the old style robes and caftans of the religious Sephardim on the streets. Of course, by the time the 1930s came, the distance between the Sephardim and Ashkenazim was not as great as it had been before the First World War. It wasn't dress, it was fear of fascism that brought us together. People were truly afraid.

Albahari's parents remained alert. By the middle 1930s Jewish refugees from the north began arriving in Yugoslavia. Zagreb bore the brunt, but some refugees made it to Sarajevo, where La Benevolencija aided with financial contributions and helped find sleeping quarters. It was these German Jews who warned Sarajevans what they could expect if the fascists took control.

Even nine year old Moris could feel the pressure building. "There was real tension in Sarajevo by the time I started school. When I was small, no one asked me what religion I was, but suddenly I was being asked if I was a Jew or not. And if I answered yes, then they would yell at me, taunt me."

In 1939 his father announced he was moving the family to Drvar, a small Serb village near the Serb-populated Krajina region of Croatia. "All my uncles said this would solve nothing, but my father thought that if something was going to happen, we would have a better chance with the Serbs than anyone else. And I recall there was a difference. Things *were* a bit easier. I was glad to leave Sarajevo."

When the war swept over Yugoslavia and Jews were rounded up in the larger cities and deported, Moris Albahari's father's decision saved their lives. "No one turned us in, no one wanted to turn us in. And when it looked like the Germans would take Dvrar, my entire family joined the Partizans." Albahari fought through the remainder of the war and returned to Sarajevo, aged 15, in 1945.

Elias Danon was born in 1915 in the house on the very corner where Austrian Archduke Franz Ferdinand had been assassinated the previous year. Danon would later marry Ljerka Brod, whose grandfather Julius had risen through the ranks of the Austrian Army to become the First Engineer-Driver of the Royal Habsburg locomotive in Bosnia. It was Julius Brod who drove the train that brought Franz Ferdinand to Sarajevo.

On a blustery afternoon I visited Elias, 77, and Ljerka, 67 years old. They lived in a rambling house overlooking the French Hospital, the destroyed parliament and the Jewish cemetery on the hill beyond. On one side of the cemetery wall were Bosnian Serb forces, on the other side the mostly Muslim Bosnian government army. I stood at the picture window staring across and squinting. Ljerka Danon gently pulled me away, pointing to a bullet hole in the far wall.

The house, which had been in Ljerka's family for generations, was a treasure chest of Habsburg and Turkish memorabilia. Exquisite Turkish rugs were spread under chandeliers of Viennese glass. A Jewish candelabra stood before a faded photograph of Ljerka's grandfather, replete in starched uniform and waxed mustache.

Over coffee and halva, which she managed to create from a war recipé cookbook, Ljerka Danon showed me Julius Brod's leather covered photograph album with its gold embossed title: Kaiserliche und Königliche Bosna Eisenbahn (The Imperial and Royal Bosnian Railroad). She brought out his white leather driving gloves. "He always wore these when driving the royal family," she said with a smile and a sigh at the same time. "He wore these the day he brought the Archduke here."

As we sat down to lunch, she said, "I'm only sorry I can't offer you more than what we have. But you know, if we had a bit more to eat, then it would be like the Second World War." She shrugged at the irony; then served a rich luncheon of stews, pickled salads and fruits from her summer garden. Fine china and crystal bowls were laid out on a lace table cloth. Considering the conditions – no gas, no running water, no electricity – it was spectacular fare. I paid my compliments. She smiled. "I am, I guess, just a Viennese leftover morsel."

As the afternoon softened and shadows stretched across the Jewish cemetery, as snipers aimed their rifles and the sharp cracks sent pedestrians scurrying over the snow covered streets, Elias Danon lit a cigarette and started speaking of his past. "My father was a textile merchant and had two stores in the center of town," he said. "Sephardic Jews dominated this market since the 1700s, and traded with other Jews in Venice and Split. They sent their goods up through the mountains to Sarajevo, into Serbia and beyond. We ourselves were relatively prosperous. I learned German not from my parents, who spoke Ladino at home, but from my governess, who looked after my brother and me."

Elias's elder brother Oskar was obsessed with music and would go on to conduct the Belgrade Symphony. Elias was groomed for the family business. "I would often go into the center of town where my father's stores were. Sarajevo was filled with Jewish shops and businesses then. The Sephardim were rather poor, you see, and most were hand workers, shoe-makers, tailors, as well as carpenters and electricians. They had stalls all through the old quarter and you can still see some of their names engraved in metal on the doors, even if the owners are all gone."

Elias Danon watched as the Nazis quickly strangled Jewish life his country. "After the occupation, the laws came quickly. We could not shop during certain hours, had to register with the police, give up our radios, wear yellow stars, and sit in our homes after 3:00 each afternoon. Jewish stores were covered with signs telling people to boycott them. I was conscripted into a labor brigade, given a shovel and sent out to work on the roads. I'm afraid to say that as we walked through the streets of Sarajevo, people would just stare at us and laugh out loud. Then my family was forced to move into a single room in our house and a German family took over the rest. I remember my mother just standing there, watching them take away everything she owned.

"In late Summer, the Ustasha took 20 men up to the old Turkish fort at Vraca, 10 Serbs, two Muslims and eight Jews – and shot them in reprisal for some act of sabotage. My father found out one of those men was his brother. He made arrangements very quickly and we slipped away a few days later, down through the mountains, through Metkovich and on to the coast. We arrived in Split and immediately set about looking for a ship to Italy." Although the port city had swollen with refugees looking desperately for any way out of the country, the Danons were lucky and by December they had arranged passage. At the last moment Oskar decided to stay and join the Partizans.

Itzhak Levi learned the price for dawdling. He told me of his family's history in Bosnia one still afternoon near Jerusalem in his flat in Mevezerret Ziyyon Absorption Center. While his two grandchildren were off at school, the thin, bronzed 77-year-old spoke of how as a young man working in the family print shop in Tuzla, he kept telling his father all through 1939 and 1940 they should get out of Yugoslavia. But his father didn't want to leave. How can we go, he asked his fretful son, when we have our homes here, our families, our friends? True enough, Levi's family had gotten along for

BINUN H. MOISE 41   ATIJAS I. SARA 36

ABINUN S. HANA 70   ABINUN S. SIMHA

ABINUN M. ABRAHAM 40   ABINUN M.

M 74   ABINUN R. SIMHA 54   ABINUN R

55   ABINUN S. HANA 56   ABINUN S

52   ABINUN S. MOISE 48   ALTARAC J.

HA 11   ABINUN I. MOSO 78   ABINUN I.

ALAMON 41   ABINUN A. MOISE 35   ABI

ABINUN J. ISAK 46   ABINUN

RIFKA 23   BINUN S. MAZALTA 25

KLARA 16   ABINUN S. AVRAM 34

ESTER 51   ABINUN D. DAVID 63   ABI

D. BERTA 30   ABINUN D. KLARA 25

ABINUN B. RAFAEL 43   ABIN

A. SAMUEL 72   ABINUN A. ISAK 56   ABI

A. RUBEN 42   ABINUN A JESUA 40

UN J. AVRAM 36   ABINUN J. LEA 29   AB

AT
ATIJAS R. MORD
ATIJAS M. MIHA

BINUN I. DONA 32   ABINUN S. JOS
   ABINUN S. LUNA 47   JOSEF 31   ABI
KOV 35   ABINUN M.   R. FLORA 28   AB
1ERJAM 37   ABINUN   SALAMON 69   A
TER 23   ABINUN M.   JAKOV 45   ABIN
FKA 53   ABINUN S.   M. SAMUEL 49
BRAHAM 64   ABINUN M.   J. JAKOV 53   ABI
S. ISAK 46   ABINUN   J. RIFKA 31   AB
 AVRAM 49   ABINUN   J. RIFKA 31   AB
BINUN S. JUDA 36   ABINUN S. AVRAM
NUN S. JOSEF 28   ABINUN M. HANA
N D. ROZA 47   ABINUN D. AVRAM 37
   ABINUN B. AVRAM 49   ABINUN S. JO
B. ISAK 38   ABINUN B. ISRAEL 37   AB
N I. SALAMON 44   ABINUN I. SARA 38
NUN A. SALAMON 33   ABINUN S. JAKO
N S. JOS 60   ABINUN S. BEJA 51

            ABINUN S ROZA 48
       ABINUN D. AVRAM 76   AB
    ATIJAS B. SARA 77   ATIJAS B. I
AS B. LEA 47   ATIJAS B. KLARA 48
HAJ 57   ATIJAS M. RAFAEL 78   AT
55   ATIJAS R. AVRAM 40   ATIJAS

generations with their Bosnian neighbors in this bustling, industrial town. His mother, an Ashkenaz, agreed with her husband. So Itzhak Levi kept working, and spent his free time at the Tuzla Jewish community center, which they called the Verein, concentrating on what he liked most: sports. On weekends, he and his friends rode their bicycles through the mountains along the Tinja River and into Brcko to meet other Jewish teenagers.

When the occupation came to Tuzla, Itzhak Levi was taken from his family and conscripted into a labor brigade in the Italian zone. From there he escaped to join the Communist Partizans and did much of his fighting in Bosnia. "We were badly under-armed but what we could do was strike and run. We had spies in many towns who would keep their ears open for news of the Germans and they would alert us when they'd be coming through with their convoys. We'd take our positions, do our best, then run for it."

Of those Sarajevo Jews who were not deported or who did not join the Partizans, some turned to their non-Jewish friends for help. Before the war, Josef Kabilio was a plumbing contractor and had a small factory within a large plant owned by Mustafa Hardaga. Hardaga, a colorful, expansive Muslim, dabbled in real estate and imported Oriental goods from Arab, Turkish, and Persian lands for sale in his stores in Sarajevo, Budapest and Prague. His young wife Zeyneba ran their home, a large Turkish-style dwelling built around a garden. Forty of his most treasured Persian carpets decorated its rooms. Kabilio visited often the Hardagas and they shared a warm and genuine friendship. When her husband was off on his lengthy trips to Istanbul or Budapest, Zeyneba would seek the advice of Josef Kabilio.

Not long after the Germans occupied Sarajevo, Mustafa Hardaga went to inspect his properties. He found Josef Kabilio hiding there. Hardaga insisted he come home with him, even though sheltering Jews would mean certain death for all if they were caught. Over the next few months, Josef Kabilio made two separate attempts to flee Sarajevo, was caught both times, escaped his jailers and returned by night to the Hardaga home. At one point while imprisoned, he was clamped into a labor brigade. By chance Zeyneba Hardaga spotted him on the street and brought food to him and his colleagues.

"When Joseph left us for the third time, all we could do was pray and hope," she said. "Later when my children asked why did you do this, I always answered what my husband said, 'You do not abandon your friends.'"

When the war ended in the Spring of 1945, Moris Albahari, Elias Danon, Itzhak Levi, and Josef Kabilio returned to Sarajevo. The world they had been born into was no more, and each of them set about building a new one.

"Of all my uncles and aunts and cousins, me and my immediate family were the only survivors," Moris Albahari recalled softly. "And our story is not unique. It certainly wasn't easy to rebuild a Jewish community after this tragedy, but we had to. We had a youngsters section for both play and study – Hebrew and regular courses. We had a summer camp in the hills. This people needed just to get their health back and we had 150–200 children to work with.

"What I did like in those days was the fact that the government made everyone work together, meaning no more differences between people. I know because for the first time in my life, I was like everybody else. No yellow stars, no one calling you dirty Jew. And people who tried to stir up nationalist troubles went straight to jail. I went on to study and became a pilot. I got married to a Jewish woman, Ela Rachela. She survived the war in Italy. We had a son David. Later I became a pilot's teacher, then went on to study machinery engineering. My specialty was building airports and I was in charge of the runway at Sarajevo's airport."

Elias Danon and his family were living in Switzerland in 1945. "My mother could not bring herself to return to Sarajevo. She could not face the destruction of the community and the confiscation of everything she had. My father and she talked it over, then decided they would never go back. They were able to go to America and moved to Michigan. She never came back to Bosnia, and they are both buried over there." Danon, who had been trained before the war to take over a large and successful business that was confiscated by the fascists, then nationalized by the communists, went into management in an international trading company. He married Ljerka Brod, rejoined the Jewish community and became a member of the communist party. "I was so used to people asking me if I was a this or that, when I first went to a party meeting, I said I'm not a Croat or a

Bosnian or a Serb, I'm a Jew, so if that's a problem, I'm not joining. The man looked up at me and said he didn't give a damn what I was. That was refreshing to hear."

Itzhak Levi returned to Tuzla, desperate to find his family. He tried to trace their path, hoping that maybe somewhere he might find them alive. He learned the Jews were deported from Tuzla beginning in May 1941. A friend said that someone told him that in a rail yard in Croatia, one man refused to leave his wife and daughter and was executed on the spot. It was thought that was a man named Levi from Tuzla.

Levi found records showing that his mother and sister entered the Djakovo concentration camp in Croatia, not far from Osijek. This was a camp used primarily for women and children. Some were shot, others tortured, most were simply denied food and starved to death. The camp bears the dubious distinction of being the only concentration camp where each grave is individually marked. But Levi found no record that his sister and mother died there. In February 1942 the camp was closed and all surviving women and children were sent to another camp, Stara Gradiska, the men to Jasenovac. Here the trail ended.

Haunted, he returned to Tuzla. Keeping to himself, he drank, he brooded, he drank. A young Muslim woman, Vahida Obar Öavin, met Levi, listened to his stories and sympathized with him. They fell in love. He stopped looking and he stopped drinking. Vahida married him, although she knew her own family would turn her out. The Jew and the Muslim, two souls now without families, moved to Sarajevo and started a family of their own.

Soon after they arrived in the Bosnian capital Vahida Levi went with her husband to the Jewish community center. She had never been inside one nor a synagogue, but she was deeply moved to see how these Jews, who had suffered so much so recently, were energetically re-building everything they could. She decided even before she had the first of her five children that she would raise them as Jews.

When peace came in 1945, Zeyneba and Mustafa Hardaga fretted and wondered over the fate of Josef Kabilio. "He had not had great luck trying to get out of Sarajevo," said Zeyneba Hardaga. "But he was a lucky young man to have escaped the Germans twice, that much is sure." One spring evening Zeyneba and Mustafa Hardaga were sitting in their garden when there was a knock on the door. It was Josef Kabilio. He had just walked back into Sarajevo. He had gone directly to his house, but it had been plundered. Again he came to the Hardagas, and again they opened their door to him. After setting himself up in business again, Josef Kabilio decided to leave Sarajevo for Israel in 1948. He promised to write often, as did Zeyneba Hardaga. Soon the first letter arrived from the middle east. There would scores to follow, stretching like a paper bridge across the decades.

[1] For a detailed look at the activities of the Italian Force in Croatia, see Jonathan Steinberg's *All or Nothing: The Axis and the Holocaust.*
[2] Fourth Exodus of the Jews. War Crimes Investigation Bureau, Sarajevo 1992, editor Major Dizdar. Also see *The Sarajevo Hagaddah:* A Study, by Dr Eugen Werber, Svetlost Publishing House, Sarajevo, 1988.
[3] Based on letters of eye witnesses and survivors now in the Archives of the American Jewish Joint Distribution Committee, New York.

PALIM ŽRTVAMA FAŠI
EJSKA OPŠTINA SARAJEVO
I ZIDOVI GOV
ORE POKOL
VIMA.
ZNAJU S
RAMOTU I
U SIVU.
I NE ZABOR
DJEČJE IGR
LJUBAVI ZA
SESTRE IZN
MAJKE UBIJ
I NE ZAB
VII 1941 – 5.VII
KADA SU
NTRACIONI LO
ZA DJEC
OG PORIJEKL
SLILE SU SE
MJESTA EVR
U UZAVRELOM
PODNEBLJU XX
REDNJEVJEKOVNIH
PRIZORA NA K
ADIVALE.
I GOVORE O
RCIMA KOJA
NAŠIM SRCI
AGU STIJENE.
KOLEKTIV
U ĐAKOVU 2.VII 1961. GOD
ONICE ĐAKOVO

Reconstruction

In the first decade of communist rule, the Yugoslav authorities severely restricted all religious groups from practicing. Because the Catholic church had a disconcertingly large number of collaborators in the *Ustasha*, its clergy and their activities were the first to be targeted. Serbian Orthodox church leaders also curried little favor with party ideology. The authorities banned Muslim presses, Islamic schools, and courts. They forbade women to wear veils after 1950 and it became a criminal office to teach children inside a mosque.

Jews were not excluded from the crackdown. Religious instruction and the study of Hebrew was forbidden, thus ensuring a rapid demise of religious observance amongst the young. Those who wanted to leave in order to lead an observant Jewish life could do so. When Israel was founded in 1948 many Yugoslav Jews chose emigration. By 1952, approximately 7,000, half the community, had left the country.

Those Jews who remained – approximately 6,500, with one third each in Zagreb, Belgrade and Sarajevo – stayed because they either tacitly agreed with the system, or believed they had nowhere else to go. Many Jews felt beholden to Tito and his *Partizans* for saving their lives, and would not argue with his policies. More than a few of those remaining married outside the religion and turned their backs on their communities.

Of Sarajevo's eight synagogues, only one, the Ashkenazi synagogue on the banks of the Miljacka River, was salvaged and it was suddenly too large for the number of observant Jews who used it. After the war, the great Sephardic synagogue was given to the city as a theater. Il Kal Grande became the Jewish Museum of Bosnia and Hercegovina, but the paucity of its collections illustrated how much had either been stolen or destroyed.

As the few remaining rabbis in the country died off, they were not replaced. Many people thought that they were seeing the end of Jewish life on south Slav soil.

Until 1967, that is, when Israel's army and air force stunned the world with their decisive victory against surrounding Arab states in a scant six days. All Communist countries save Romania severed diplomatic relations with Israel and launched virulent anti-Zionist campaigns. Even though Yugoslavia lay outside the Warsaw Pact, its non-aligned policy favored the Arabs. When federal Yugoslav printing presses started churning out anti-Israel agitprop, highly assimilated Yugoslav Jews suddenly felt themselves riding between two horses. They may not have felt very Jewish, but many had family in Israel. Others simply could not bring themselves to condemn the Jewish homeland. Further, like Jews around the world, many Yugoslav Jews took pride in Israel's victory.

"This was the turning point for us," Dr Ladoslav Kadelburg said in his Belgrade office in 1986. Kadelburg, then president of the Jewish Federation of Yugoslavia, went on. "Young people whose parents never brought them to the community were now asking for information about Israel, Judaism, Jewish holidays, culture. They wanted to learn Hebrew. They wanted to get involved. And it was this younger generation that turned everything around for us." In fact, this younger generation soon began taking over the communities themselves.

By the 1980s, Joint representatives could hardly keep up with the programming requests that emanated from Zagreb, Belgrade, and Sarajevo. Zagreb wanted to open a new kindergarten and did so in 1989. Belgrade expanded its cultural programs, and Sarajevo taught a group of 13 year old boys the rudiments of Hebrew so they could be bar mitzvahed together. Jewish youth groups traipsed off to visit each others' communities and assembled each November for a four-day conference. In 1989, 110 people between 15 to 25 years of age attended. At the Makkabia sports weekend later that year on the island of Hvar, 650 Jews from all six republics came.

The federation's summer camp at Pirovac on the Adriatic was welcoming Jews from hardline socialist countries as well as those from home. When Czech and Bulgarian Jews saw people dancing the hora, singing Hebrew songs, and found a dining hall filled with Israeli flags, they were stunned. Their governments still perpetuated anti-Israel propaganda and this kind of activity would have landed them in jail. One Czech Jew said when a diplomat came to Prague from Jerusalem, the foreign ministry had to send someone to Vienna to purchase an Israeli flag.

Throughout Yugoslavia, relations were excellent between Jews and their fellow citizens. A Serb-Israel Friendship Society was established in Belgrade. The Musejski Prostor Museum in Zagreb curated a blockbuster exhibition entitled "The Jews of Yugoslavia." It later traveled to Belgrade, Novi Sad, Sarajevo, and New York.

Jews in Tito's Yugoslavia attained top positions in television, the arts, academia, literature, governmental ministries, as well as the legal and medical professions. In no other post-Holocaust socialist country (save perhaps Hungary) had Jews climbed to such heights. Yugoslavia's best known novelist, Danilo Kis, was Jewish, and short story writer David Albahari and novelist Anna Somlo were both on the Belgrade Jewish community board. Sculptor Nandor Glid's mammoth creations commemorating the Holocaust were sent to Israel and Germany. Some of the country's most successful businessmen were Jews and the armed forces had Jewish generals. All rather staggering considering there were but 6,500 in a country of 23 million.

Sarajevo continued with its eclectic mix. A Muslim, Dr Muhamed Nezirovich, became the foremost authority on Bosnian Jewish history, and a Jew, Nada Bojanich, was Bosnia's leading Arabist. One day in 1988, a young man of 17, a Bosnian Serb by the name of Ranko Jajcanin, came to the Jewish community. He approached a table of elderly Jewish men and asked if they could help him learn more about Judaism. They thought him amusing at first and they began to chat. It was soon clear he knew more than they did. Jajcanin went on to win a competition on Bible Studies in Israel and the community hired him to travel around Bosnia and Dalmatia to conduct religious services, which he had somehow taught himself. In 1990 the community aided Jajcanin in his conversion to Judaism and helped him secure grants from Joint and the Doron Foundation so he could move to Israel and train for the rabbinate.

Itzhak Levi's daughter Rachela grew up within the Jewish community, as did Moris Albahari's son David. So did Ivan Ceresnjes, Jakob Finci, and Danilo Nikolich. They knew each other well and as they grew older and married, they brought their own children to the community. Rachela's two sons, Haris, born in 1981 and Denis, born in 1984, came less often than most, but still managed to peddle by on their bicycles. "Before they took me away from Sarajevo when the war started," Haris said in Israel in 1994, "I never knew who was a Jew, a Muslim, a Croat, or a Serb. And the funny thing is, when I think back to those days, I still don't know."

Josef Kabilio had been living in Israel since 1948. He had married, had children and grandchildren. His wife had since died. In Sarajevo, Mustafa Hardaga took to his bed in the late 1940s with a failing heart and did not recover. His businesses had already been nationalized and he had lost his stores in Prague and Budapest. As he lay there debilitated and without strength until his death in 1955, his wife Zyneba quietly sold off their possessions. After his death, she sold their home and in 1957 remarried. Her daughter Aida was born a year later and her husband died soon after. Throughout the 1970s and 1980s, a childhood leg injury resurfaced and kept Zyneba Hardaga hospitalized for months on end. With thrombosis setting in, the leg was amputated in 1980. She was bedridden for a year.

She never wrote a word of this to Kabilio, even though the two exchanged frequent letters, addressing each other as "My dearest sister," and "My dearest brother." She wrote to ask for advice about the children, education, insurance, but never let on about her failing health. Kabilio closed every letter by asking her to come to Israel so they could sit together in his garden, drink Turkish coffee and talk about the old times, before the war.

Josef Kabilio was also keeping something from Zyneba Hardaga. He had heard that Yad Vashem,

Sarajevans Milan Hamovich and Rosita Danon at the Yugoslav Jewish summer camp on the Croatian coast. July 1988.

Israel's Holocaust museum, gave special citations to non-Jews who went to extraordinary lengths during the Second World War to save Jewish lives. They were given awards and a tree was planted in their honor on the Avenue of Righteous Gentiles. Although well into his 80s, he went to the museum several times to speak with those in charge of these awards. He heard that substantiation would be needed, interviews had to be made and the facts and dates checked. There were other claims ahead of his and only so many investigators. Perhaps something else was blocking the way. He was asking that this award be granted to a Muslim, something that had never been done before.

When Josef Kabilio turned 88 in 1985, Zeyneba Hardaga received a letter from Yad Vashem. They informed her of the award and that she would be flown to Jerusalem to receive it. Seven months later, a stunned Josef Kabilio watched Zeyneba Hardaga being helped off an airplane. "You never told me!" he complained, looking at her cane. "And you never told me what you were up to, either," she said with a scolding smile.

Zeyneba Hardaga received her award and helped plant her tree. She stayed in Jerusalem a month. While traffic hissed past outside his door, and his grandchild played not far away, every morning and every afternoon, the 88-year-old Jew and the 69-year-old Muslim sat in the garden, drinking Turkish coffee and talking away the hours. Josef Kabilio was 92 when he died in 1989. Three years later, war broke out in Sarajevo. This time it was Zeyneba Hardaga who was in need of rescue.

The Shadow of War, II

Every year on the first Friday in June, just before dawn, Mladan Swarz strolled through the baroque center of Ljubljana and caught the morning train for Belgrade. About that time, on the Adriatic coast, Mimi Ferrara would leave her apartment under the old stone walls of Dubrovnik. She rode a bus along the coast to Split, and in a small syna-

Graves of Sarajevo children killed by Croatian fascists during the Second World War. May 1989.

gogue in the city's medieval heart, she met Edo Tauber. Together they headed for the airport, just around the time Srdan Matic was boarding the Belgrade-bound train in Zagreb's neo-Rococo station.

Others headed for Belgrade as well: from dusty Balkan backwaters in Macedonia and Montenegro, from Bosnian towns where mosques and minarets dominated the cityscape, and from Austro-Hungarian river cities along the Sava and Drava rivers. Together these two dozen men and women, well educated, erudite, and proudly Jewish, came to represent their tiny communities at the annual meeting of the Federation of Jewish communities in Yugoslavia. The proceedings were laced with jokes and constant interruptions for meals, snacks and drinks.

Or so it had gone for forty years. But as Jacob Finci flew from Sarajevo to Belgrade with three of his colleagues in June, 1991, he wondered how much good will would be found around the table this time. Six weeks before the annual meeting came the first armed clashes between Serb and Croat civilians and para-military units. Two weeks previously Croatia held a referendum endorsing independence.

In the past, there had been an occasional trickle of nationalist sentiment seeping into Jewish gatherings. This year, from the opening gavel it flooded the rooms and drowned the spirit of camaraderie that had existed since 1945. "It was clear from the beginning this would all go nowhere," Finci said. Meetings sank like swamped paper boats, drowned in accusations. Intolerance reigned. This time, there were no jokes to lighten the proceedings. "The mood was dark and depressing," Finci recalled. "Each night, the four of us from Sarajevo would sit alone in a café with Mladan from Ljubljana. We drank our coffee and went over the possibilities for Yugoslavia. None of them looked good."

After the annual meeting it was customary for all Yugoslav Jewish communities to meet in Djakovo, the World War Two Croatian concentration camp where those killed during the Holocaust are buried in a Jewish cemetery. The ceremony in 1991 fell on a balmy, early summer day. Over 150 Jews came from all six republics and their dust-caked chartered buses waited in the parking lot.

A military band played somber marches. Rabbi Zadik Danon from Belgrade chanted prayers. Afterwards, in single file, everyone made their way past the tombstones, then headed for a corner of the cemetery where the graves of Jewish children and infants lie.

The small metal signs, barely knee-high, told the same story thirty-three times. Hanah Kalderon, eight months old, Rahel Atijas, one month old, Izi Papo, one month old, Jozef Klein, two months old, David Izrael, three years old. Nearly all of them had been born in Sarajevo.

Children carry with them the future of every ethnic group, its hopes and promises. But the 20th century has denied the Jews of Central and Eastern Europe much of a future. The death of 1,500,000 children during the Holocaust saw to that. Here in Djakovo, once each year, a handful of Yugoslav Jews came quietly face to face with this tragedy. A half century after the fact, some still wept.

This year the traumatic prospect of a new war was as close as the parking lot. Rough-looking men dressed in crude military gear, bellies protruding over their pants, were sitting on cars, selling Kalashnikov rifles. The asking price was 300 German marks.

After the service, the Sarajevo community bus headed south across Croatia, over the Sava river plain, past scores of the republic's newly-adopted flag displaying the Sahovnica, Croatia's age-old red and white checkerboard heraldic symbol. "It was less than comforting to see it," Finci said. "This is exactly the same flag the Ustasha used in the Second World War, the same flag that flew over Djakovo when so many Jews were murdered, only then it had a big U in the center. Of course things aren't the same in the 1990s as then, and Croats today can't be blamed for this period, but still, seeing this flag sent shivers down my spine." Watching the flags go by, Finci believed war was imminent between Croatia and Serbia, "but none of us thought we would see war in Bosnia, not with Serbs, Croats, Muslims, and Jews living not only in the same towns, but in the same buildings and mixed up in the same families."

The second week of July, Ivan Ceresnjes, president of the Sarajevo community, went to the Jewish Federation's summer camp in Pirovac on the Adriatic coast. This was the family session, and the 50-odd guests, ranging from infants to grandparents, had come from Belgrade, Zagreb, Sarajevo, as well as Osijek, Subotica, and elsewhere.

The Adriatic coast was as crowded and noisy as it always was in summer. Until Sunday 14 July, that is. "The children were out on their rafts and plastic boats and we were sitting on the terrace overlooking the water," said Ceresnjes. "Suddenly there was a huge roar like thunder getting nearer and nearer. JNA (Yugoslav National Army) fighters swooped in formation overhead, flying low and roaring straight over the mountains toward Krajina. For a moment we were silent, then everyone ran for the radios and television. This was the beginning of the real hostilities. One woman from Belgrade stood up and shouted that she had to go to the front lines to help her brother and sister Serbs. It was her sacred duty, she screamed. Then a man who sympathized with the Croats said he wanted to do the same for Croatia. They went at each other and finally I told them both to shut up.

"We went to the telephone and called the Jewish communities in Belgrade and Zagreb. I met with the parents and we decided to stay, at least for the day, to wait things out. We had dinner and the children went back to their playing. We adults sat on the terrace. All the while, the highway on the edge of town was lined with cars. Every one with foreign license plates was heading north, out of Yugoslavia. Every car with plates from Nis, Belgrade, Titograd was heading south. I had my last cigarette on the terrace just after midnight and still the cars were bumper to bumper, slowly moving, like a river of headlights."

By morning the highway was empty. Ceresnjes and a few others walked into the town center. What had been a bustling sea side resort was now deserted. "We discussed things and decided we may as well stay for the rest of the week.

"Not so many people argued any more. We listened to the conflicting reports on radio and TV. Serbs heard what they wanted to hear and Croats heard their version, but people were quiet about it. The children had a great time, it was hot, we took our naps, grilled fish for dinner, and by the end of the week we were all nice and sunburned. Then we packed our bags, locked up the villa and drove home to our separate republics. And that was the final meeting of the Jews in a country called Yugoslavia."

Because Slovenia had practically no Serbs living within its borders, this northernmost republic quickly and successfully extricated itself from the dying Federation of Yugoslavia. When Croatia declared full independence, the well-armed 600,000 ethnic Serbs within its borders went on the offensive and war raged between Croatia and Serbia until a cease fire prevailed at the end of 1991. By then, Croatia had lost nearly a third of its territory.

Bosnia-Hercegovina did not escape the rising tide of nationalism. On 15 October, the Republic declared sovereignty. A few days later, the Serbs living in Bosnia declared they were now represented solely by their own parliament.

Finci was now convinced that war would come and the Jews of Sarajevo readied their community. "We called a meeting of all Jewish doctors in town," Finci said. "Fifteen came and we asked them to make a list of what we'd need. No one thought we were overreacting. One young doctor added something no one else thought of: body bags. Everyone laughed, perhaps nervously, and we said, 'don't make such black jokes!' He looked at us and said, 'you'll see, you'll see.'"

It was at this time Tuvya Raviv, representative of the Jewish Agency for Israel, entered the picture. Born in Serbia before the Second World War, he and his family had survived the Holocaust by hiding with false papers in Hungary. More than once, Raviv's life was spared – or made considerably safer – by someone's act of kindness, and these experiences left their mark upon him.

Raviv emigrated to Israel in 1948, became a highly decorated colonel in the army, and later became manager of the largest department store in Jerusalem. After two heart attacks he changed careers, joined the Zionist-oriented Jewish Agency for Israel, and moved to Budapest to help foster the rebirth of Jewish life there. But Raviv soon became alarmed as nearby Yugoslavia started disintegrating and he began visiting Jewish communities there as well. Each month he rented a car and drove off to meet with one, two, sometimes dozens of concerned parents in Serbia, Macedonia, Croatia, Slovenia, and Bosnia. At first, very few people wanted to meet with him. But Raviv was patient as well as determined. And he kept coming back, always with the same message. He began his meetings with these words, "There's going to be a war here. I'm offering you a way out now." By the time the war began in Sarajevo, Tuvya Raviv had made 15 Federation-wide trips, logged nearly 10,000 miles, held 30 meetings and had spoken with over 500 Yugoslav Jews.

It was Raviv who insisted Finci write to every community member in September 1991 – a half year before the siege – and advise them to get their passports in order and apply for Israeli visas. Four hundred Jews responded immediately, and the community center started making lists.

These precautions were discovered by Oslobodjenja, the daily Sarajevo newspaper. Finci said, "their article ended by saying that surely it's a bad sign if the Jews are wishing to leave, because they have a certain sense about danger."

'When the Jews are leaving, it is a bad sign for the city.' This has long been a Bosnian expression, and since that autumn in 1991, one could hear it every time Sarajevo's Jews arranged their convoys and left. It is poignant and it is sad, although it isn't true. The Holocaust proved that. But it goes back deeper into Bosnian history than this century. Jews had found their place here in this Balkan river valley and although they were in one sense outsiders, they became part of its society. They were accepted and they returned the favor with loyalty and affection. 'When the Jews are leaving, it is a bad sign for the city.' Finci heard it from the President's office the day the first Jewish community air convoy left Sarajevo. 'Not you, not the *Jews*,' one of the president's aides told him by telephone.

That autumn, in every Jewish household in Sarajevo, where the memory of the Holocaust lived with its survivors and their offspring, the love of home faced off against the instinct for survival. Decisions would have to be made, and quickly. Jacob and Nada Finci sat down with their 19 year old son Alan, who had just spent the summer in Israel. "We had a family meeting, with my 14 year old son Asher as well. Alan asked about what I thought would happen in Bosnia and if he should stay. I took a breath and said, for the first time in front of the family, that war was coming. He could stay if he wanted, but he would have to be prepared to go into the Army. And he would have to be willing to kill his friends. Alan made up his mind to go to Israel, and Asher would go with him."

During these final months before war swept over Bosnia, La Benevolencija was one of the most active religious-based organizations in the country. It planned new publications and art exhibitions. For the Sarajevo Winter Festival that began in January, it produced eight of the 28 performances under the banner "Shalom Sarajevo – Jews to the beloved City." But the shadow of war was stretching over Bosnia.

On 15 January 1992 the sovereignty of Croatia and

Slovenia was recognized by the European Union. The government of President Alija Izetbegovic called for a referendum on Bosnia-Hercegovina's independence. Serbs boycotted the polls, Muslims and Croats voted for it overwhelmingly. Results were announced on 2 March and Bosnian Serb forces put up barricades that day. Bosnian government forces erected their own 48 hours later. On 27 March Radovan Karadzic declared the Serb Republic of Bosnia.

On 6 April the European Union recognized Bosnia-Hercegovina and a rally against war was held in the square between the Holiday Inn and the Parliament. Well over 50,000 citizens attended; some say only Muslims and Croats showed up, others claim all three ethnic groups were in evidence. Bosnian Serb snipers opened fire on the crowd from the Holiday Inn across the street and Bosnian police stormed the building with grenades. Eleven people died that day. War had come. The preparations the Jewish community had started needed to be put into action immediately.

Death notices in the Sarajevo daily newspaper, Oslobodjena. January 1994.

Joint's country director for Yugoslavia Yechiel Bar-Chaim contacted their special representative Eli Eliezri. Eliezri, a compact, middle-aged Israeli, had helped Joint with rescue operations in Ethiopia and Iran. He flew to Belgrade while Bar-Chaim telephoned the Sarajevo community leadership. Get your list in order, he told them. Now.

Eliezri turned to Jasha Bienenfeld, a successful Zagreb businessman and active Jewish community member with strong ties to the JNA. Bienenfeld and Eliezri were joined in their efforts by the Belgrade Jewish community. The Croatian Jew and the Serb Jews may have had differences between them, but they joined forces to help Bosnia's Jews. Together they rented a plane from the JNA which was scheduled to fly to Sarajevo on 10 April at 10:00 am.

Using the only two phones in the community center, Finci and his colleagues went to work, calling every name on the list. One of the calls went to Itzhak Levi and his children's families. Weak from a recent heart attack, Levi crossed through the city's road blocks to meet with everyone in his daughter Rachela's apartment. Levi, who had lost one family to war already, began by saying they would have to act fast. It was time to, grab the children and leave.

Every one of his children replied that Levi was getting carried away. How could they leave their homes, their friends, their families? Stupefied, Itzhak Levi broke down and cried. Between sobs he said, "Why, why is this happening to me again? Why is this all being played out before my eyes, the same as last time?"

The entire family argued with him but the old man would not budge. He finally said, "You can do whatever you wish. Stay if you want to because I can't make you leave. But here's what I will do. Either I will remain here, and that will kill me, or you'll give me the grandchildren and let me take them to safety."

His daughter Rachela Dzidic said, "My husband Atif was on a business trip outside Sarajevo. He was desperate to get in, I had my father who wanted to get out with my sons, nieces and nephews. What choice did I have? Of course I thought he was overreacting. I couldn't stand to see my children leave, but after all, I kept assuring myself this would all be over in a couple of weeks."

Five pick-up points were set up around the city, and buses rented by the Jewish community began their journey before dawn, driving through a city living on its nerve ends. By the first week of April the airport road had turned into a snipers' shooting gallery and Ceresnjes and Finci had asked all warring factions to allow the Jewish community buses free access, which they did. That did not stop everyone on those buses from holding their breath during that long 10-minute drive through the suburbs toward the airport. On those buses were the children of Danilo Nikolich, Jacob Finci, and Rachela Dzidic. As they arrived, a single plane from Belgrade landed and took off. On that plane was Atif Dzidic, the father of Haris and Denis. He made his way gingerly from the airport back into town, and found only Rachela at home, sitting in the living room, crying. Atif Dzidic did not even get to say good-bye to his sons.

At the airport, the Jewish community plane did not arrive on time. "The airport was like the pictures I'd seen of the fall of Saigon," Ceresnjes said. "Six television crews were walking around the lounges. Their cameras looked like metal birds of prey, feeding on the fear."

Hours went by and Ceresnjes frantically phoned and ran between the Army control tower and the buses. Working alongside was Gus Konturas, a Greek/Dutch/American employed by the International Rescue Committee who had thrown himself into the task of helping get Sarajevo's Jews out of Bosnia.

Just after 2:00 PM, the sun caught the glint of the wings of a white Boeing 707, which touch-

Man running across a bridge exposed to sniper fire. February 1994.

ed down, turned toward the airport and came to a halt. Two sets of stairs were rolled out and the community's buses began unloading. But before people reached the plane, a set of doors in the airport burst open, and families of JNA officers stormed up the stairs of the plane. Ceresnjes watched in horror, running this way and that to try and halt the onslaught.

"We managed to stop at least half of them, and got some of our people on board. We had some hysterical people on our hands. I ran for the telephone and managed to get hold of the JNA command at the Belgrade airport. I yelled, they yelled back." Bienenfeld and the Belgrade leadership was told what happened and went to work as well. "It took only an hour," Ceresnjes said, "before two Tupelovs came flying in from Bihac and our people finally boarded the plane. I went home, completely exhausted. But we had gotten 362 people out of Sarajevo that day."

As snipers took up their positions closer to the town center and mortar shells tore into the city,

another air convoy was arranged for 17 April. Few missed the irony. This was the first day of Passover, the Jewish holiday commemorating the Jewish Exodus from Egypt. It was also a miserable, gray day, and a steady rain had fallen since morning. Eliezri, Bienenfeld, and Serb Jewish leaders helped arrange matters at the Belgrade airport. Ceresnjes, again aided by Konturas and his reams of permissions and manifests, managed the Sarajevo end. Two hundred Sarajevans boarded another rented plane, then Ceresnjes and Konturas asked one of the bus drivers to drop them off at the community. It was time for the Passover Seder.

Normally up to 100 Jews and their friends came for the first night of Passover. Tables were covered with linen, silver ceremonial objects brought out and laid at the head of the table. This year, seven people showed up.

"This was one of the saddest nights of my life, because as we read the story of the Exodus from Egypt, we all knew the heart of our community was already gone. Everything we had built over the past forty years had come to an end. Whatever else we would have from this point on," said Ceresnjes, "it would be a different community, a war community."

The museums of Sarajevo were packed away. Curators, ticket clerks, guards, and directors worked together, slipping pictures off hooks, unlocking cabinets. They carefully wrapped pottery and ceramics, heaved open old storage crates and watched as their treasures were loaded onto trucks and driven to safety. At the State Museum of Bosnia-Hercegovina, curators once again took the Sarajevo Hagaddah out of its case and delivered it to a still-secret location. Only Ceresnjes would be allowed to visit it.

On 21 April 20 mortar rounds crashed into the city's television station. Another wave of community members and their friends beseeched Finci and Ceresnjes to arrange a third airlift. On 1 May Konturas saw to it that 171 Sarajevans left on the third air convoy, of whom 80 were community members.

The Jewish Museum of Bosnia-Hercegovina has been housed, since the 1960s, in Il Kal Grande, the old Sephardic synagogue destroyed by the Nazis in 1941. During the siege of Sarajevo by the Bosnian Serbs, the collections were placed in crates and the windows filled with sand bags. January 1994.

43

Altogether three airlifts had evacuated 731 Sarajevans, 40 % of whom were non-Jews.

As they watched the plane arch upwards and toward Belgrade, Finci and Ceresnjes went with friends to a café in the town center. "It was a Friday, a wonderful, sunny day," said Finci, "and the first really hot day of the year. No snipers shot. No mortars were fired. It was also a holiday. While we sat there, a few people started saying that we had really gone too far, that we Jews had made fools of ourselves. Everything was about to calm down, they said, just like it had in Croatia. Actually, some people were a little angry with me, saying we had overreacted. I said nothing but wondered if they might be right."

The following day Finci went to the community center as usual. A few elderly men were upstairs praying in the synagogue. Other members were sitting in the lounge chatting. "Around 11:00 I left to go home and have lunch with Nada. I crossed the bridge and walked past the Army's Cultural House. JNA soldiers were hurriedly loading up lorries and taking things out. I moved quickly past them and turned the corner. Suddenly I was facing Bosnian government troops all over, creeping toward them. I was lucky not to be shot and as soon as I got home I ran to the phone. 'Don't leave the building, what ever you do!' At noon, the shooting began. The noise was unbelievable. Nada and I crouched down, and we dragged our bed out of the bedroom and into the hallway. We shut the door, grabbed some candles and flashlights and I said, 'well, I guess I didn't overreact after all.'"

Ceresnjes was at the community center. "The gunfire came from everywhere and the phone lines went dead. We huddled in the basement, but after a while we came up into the lounge. Tzitzko stood in his kitchen, calm as you please, making coffee and grilling meats.

"Just across the river, we saw a JNA armored truck driving by and it was hit and shelled. We watched the driver – a boy, really – fall stone dead halfway out of the cab, his arm just hanging. He stayed like that overnight and no one could do a thing.

"By evening, since the fighting was still raging, Tzitzko went back to work and made dinner. By midnight, the fighting started to die down and people fell asleep. I walked around the building most of the night. Moonlight came through the windows. I counted 60 people sleeping there. I had no idea who half of them were; just people from the neighborhood who were scared, I guess. But from that day on, we never turned anyone away.

"At 5:00 the next morning, a few of us decided to go home. It was turning light when we made those first steps outside. Smoke was drifting down the street, fires were everywhere. The first couple of blocks were deserted, with burnt cars, a dead person or two, and JNA uniforms that had been thrown off and discarded. We turned onto Titova, the main shopping street and all hell was there to see. Looters were everywhere: Serbs, Croats, Muslims. It didn't matter, they were stealing everything, plundering the stores. Police were running around, shouting and grabbing people, but it didn't do any good. Some people were walking around like sleepwalkers. They were in complete shock. Others were screaming and running from house to house looking for their children, their fathers or mothers. I was with Danilo Nikolich. We couldn't believe it. So this is how a city dies, I thought, this is how a city learns about war.

"It took an hour-and-a-half to reach home. I found my family in the hallway where they had moved their blankets and mattresses. They had spent the night with everyone else in the cellar and had just come back upstairs, but they still weren't going into any room with a window. We were so happy to find each of us alive, and we hugged and cried and laughed. I said to my wife, well, its time to get you and the kids ready to leave. But we knew even then it was going to be a lot harder than before."

Over the following few days, Ceresnjes and Finci sat in their office surrounded by pleading parents, the elderly, even children, asking them for help. But Sarajevo was now wholly surrounded and the airport was closed.

On 18 May 1992, the warring factions agreed to allow a general, non-sectarian convoy drive out of the city. It stretched 10 miles and included 80 buses and 1,000 other vehicles. Some community members left with this convoy. Others slipped over the front line or along with other Sarajevans, bought their way directly through it.

Mortars pounded the Bosnian capital while snipers firmed up the front lines. By 25 May the Red Cross reported 1,000 dead in Sarajevo hospitals and advised burning the bodies. On 27 May, a mortar landed in a line of people waiting for bread. Twenty died, 160 were wounded. Many had their feet and legs blown off. In early August, the Children's Embassy arranged a bus convoy out of Sarajevo. Two children were shot to death.

By early Autumn, working with the Zagreb Jewish community and Jasha Bienenfeld, La Benevolencija had successfully arranged five bus convoys. Bienenfeld, a towering figure with a permanent five o'clock shadow, relished negotiating with both the Croats and Bosnian Serbs in each of their respective territories. He took control of arranging buses and fuel trucks, permissions and route plans. He could be seen at all hours checking off names, yelling into mobile telephones, arguing, hurrying passengers onto buses, and wrapping his arm around the shoulder of this border guard or that commander. Working with Finci, Nikolich, and Ceresnjes, another 659 souls were brought to safety between 1 August and 15 October, only half of whom were Jewish.

All that autumn of 1992 battle lines were encroaching on the city and it was obvious the road out would soon close for good. The community decided to arranged its biggest convoy for November 1992. The list had nearly 400 names on it.

By this time, the Bosnian government controlled all exits from Sarajevo and every person on the list had to be approved by the Ministry of Interior. Because matters were becoming dicier, Joint sent Eliezri into Sarajevo for the first time to help with negotiations.

Community members and their friends scurried about the city chasing papers, stamps and forms: everything that was needed to secure legal passage from the Interior Ministry. Rachela Dzidic was one of those. She and her husband wanted to join her father and two sons, now living in Israel. It had been 7 months since they had been together. They packed, said good-bye to their neighbors and fellow office workers. Then on Friday, 13 November, Rachela telephoned the Jewish community to find out what time she had to be there to leave the following morning. She was told that for some reason, her name had been taken off the list. She was not allowed out of Sarajevo. "I listened, put the telephone down, and turned to my husband. I told him what had happened. He just stared at me. And I had a complete nervous breakdown."

The following day, 10 buses departed Sarajevo for Split without Rachela or her husband. 394 Sarajevans were taken to safety.

During the siege, the Jewish cemetery became the front line, with Bosnian Serb forces on the right side of the cemetery and Bosnian government troops facing them through the forest of white stones and grave markers. January 1994 (left).

Jews, like everyone else in Sarajevo, are buried in city parks. January 1994 (below).

A Community Goes to Work

It took several weeks for Rachela Dzidic to return to work. Atif had taken time off and stayed at home. Neighbors and friends brought food and visited. In Israel their sons Haris and Denis watched the television news with footage of Sarajevans being brought to Israel, but not their parents. Turning to his brother, Denis asked, "Are we orphans now, Haris?" Some Sarajevo adult evacuees, either with insensitivity or deliberate cruelty, told the boys their parents wanted to stay in Bosnia, but nothing was further from the truth.

The days in Sarajevo grew rapidly shorter. This year the heat did not go on, electricity did not work and water did not flow from the taps. This was one thing in summer: inconvenient, uncomfortable even. But when the first frosts came, for the elderly and the very young, matters became dangerous.

By November it was dark at 4:00 PM and snow hardened on the streets, turning to ice. Running across them was now impossible and that made it easier for snipers. There were more open spaces too because without heat, people began chopping down the trees that lined city streets and those in parks. The handworkers in the old Turkish quarter turned out tinny wood burning stoves for 200 German marks. People scurried across town to buy them, then funneled the tin exhausts out of living room windows, many of which were now just plastic sheets. Every combustible object went into these stoves: felled trees, furniture, doors, books, and shoes. Sarajevo had taken to cannabilizing itself.

UNHCR predicted 400,000 deaths in Bosnia that winter, but miraculously, the sub-freezing temperatures that often descended upon central Bosnia for months on end did not materialize. Outside Sarajevo, negotiators struggled vainly to produce a peace plan. Inside the city, people realized there would be no armed intervention on their behalf.

The news photographers, camera operators, newspaper and radio reporters were not there in advance of some greater western involvement; they had come to record the torture and execution.

Sarajevans also realized they would have to spend their days standing in line for food, bread, wood and water just to stay alive. Physicians, store clerks, bank executives, university professors, radio disc jockeys, car mechanics: everyone who did not have ready access to hard currency was driven to living off handouts from the various aid agencies. Those who did have savings in hard currency found that with potatoes at $12 per pound, meat at $18 per pound, sugar and flour at $15 per pound, and gasoline at $130 a gallon, these would quickly vanish. The average adult had lost 22 pounds by winter's end.

By Spring 1993, the Muslim-Croat alliance disappeared under a hail of bullets as the former allies turned on each other. In May, Bosnian Serbs rejected the Vance-Owen peace plan. A month later, Lord Owen urged Bosnia's Muslim-led government to acknowledge its underdog position and accept Serb-Croat proposals to divide Bosnia into 3 ethnic zones. That Summer, President Izetbegovic and Radovan Karadzic signed an accord to restore utilities in Sarajevo, but nothing came of it. That same day, twelve people lining up to fill water jugs at a public spigot died in a mortar attack.

By this time, La Benevolencija was operating at a level of efficiency and professionalism that surprised even its leaders. The entire community center had been turned into a warren of offices. More than that, the synagogue had become a beacon. It was said that the Jews knew how to get things done, could solve problems, find housing, run convoys, give out medicine. I will use my notes from one day in November 1993 to describe the community's activities during the siege.

49

Every morning before 8:00, Rashu drove his bullet-ridden Volkswagen through town to pick up Jadranka, a doctor, and Mirjana a nurse, both of whom worked in the community center's first aid clinic. He fetched me from the Holiday Inn, drove quickly along streets exposed to snipers and turned onto a pedestrian footbridge that put us out of harm's way. He puttered over the river, turned left and stopped briefly at a military checkpoint where a young soldier in woolen mittens looked over the papers before we shuddered to a halt in front of the community center on Dobrovoljacka.

Before the war, Rashu, a Muslim with a wife and two children, was an electronics engineer who came often to the community to have a coffee and sit on the terrace with old college friends. Once the war began, he sent his family to relatives in the Serb region of Vojvodina and accepted Ivan Ceresnjes's offer to become the community's 'official' driver. It gave him something to do. Afterwards, he went home to his empty apartment.

With international mail held to a standstill during the siege of Sarajevo, the Jewish community opened its own post office and brought nearly 100,000 letters in and out of the city. January 1994.

Jadranka and Mirjana, both Croats, went upstairs to work. As they entered the building they walked past a bulletin board facing the street. Tacked to it was a list of those who had letters waiting inside the community's post office. La Benevolencija's mail system was started in the summer of 1992 after international mail delivery collapsed. By the end of 1993, 76,000 letters had been taken out of Sarajevo by La Benevolencija, and 29,000 were received. The Jewish post office was so efficient that the city's postmaster also funneled sacks of mail through it.

If telephone numbers were written on the incoming envelopes, La Benevolencija volunteers, like Igor or Bojan, both teenagers and best of friends, rang up the recipients. Otherwise the names went on the bulletin board. If no one claimed the letter within seven days, someone, like Bojan, would hop on his bicycle and deliver them. "I can't say I like riding around the city," he said. "But mail is so important for people."

Bojan had good reason to fear venturing out. While playing football with friends the previous summer, a mortar shell landed near them, sending the boys diving into a doorway. After a few minutes, they ran at full speed across the field and toward the high-rise facing them, but no sooner were they underway than two shells landed, one just before them, another behind. Seven teenagers went sprawling over the grass, wounded by shrapnel. One was killed instantly. "I didn't know what hit me," Bojan said. He rolled up his pants' legs to reveal two fist-sized clumps of flesh missing behind both thighs. "The doctors told me it's a miracle I didn't lose my legs, and they operated on me without anesthetic. They gave me a pillow for me to hold over my face. I screamed for hours."

While Bojan was in the hospital, unable to move, he was told his 15 year old brother and father had been wounded while standing in line for bread. "They *never* stood together and it happened just at that second when my brother came to relieve my Dad in the queue."

For the three weeks they remained in the hospital together, Bojan's nurses rolled his bed through the halls of Kosevo Hospital, into the one working elevator, then across to the ward where his brother lay, his chest and shoulder bandaged. With his brother often asleep or sedated, Bojan would lean over and hold his hand, and be there to smile when he awoke. "Since then, my brother rarely leaves his room. He plays his guitar and reads. But he doesn't really go out much, and at the first sign of shelling he runs for the bathroom, the only room in our flat with no windows." As he rolled down his pants leg and mounted his bike, Bojan said, "As a matter of fact, I was like that for a half year. But now – " and he opened his hands wide.

Just as he was leaving, I asked Bojan if he was Jewish. He smiled. "My mother's mother was Jewish and from Croatia. Her entire family was killed in

Jasenovac concentration camp except for her husband, a Polish Catholic. My father's mother is a Bosnian Serb and his father was a Montenegran who lived in Bosnia. So what am I? Either a Bosnian milkshake or a Bosnian cocktail. Take your pick."

Behind Igor's and Bojan's post office, those coming to the community center to pick up food met with Djuro Bozovich and his mother Nada Levy. They had set up a table and office in the old breezeway between the community center and the synagogue, just in front of their warehouse full of canisters, cartons and crates of food.

Nada survived the Second World War because she came from mixed parentage. Djuro married his high school sweetheart, Natalia, a Bosnian Serb, and until this war they worked in the same engineering firm in Lukavica, which later fell behind Bosnian Serb lines. Djuro, despite a very weak heart badly in need of valve replacement (not possible in Sarajevo before or during the siege), was known to be a great fixer for the community. When they needed food sent to someone, or something purchased on the black market for the community itself, Djuro would get it done. Natalia would sometimes stop by for lunch with Djuro. In winter he slept over at the community center rather than face the steep hill up to their home, or the cold that awaited. Djuro was in his mid 40s.

Behind them was the storeroom where Novo, a Bosnian Serb, worked with Boro, a Jew. In what had once been the synagogue's social hall, boxes were stacked ten feet high: rice and beans and pasta and tinned meats and fish and vegatables and tomato sauce and crackers and cookies and flour and salt and sugar and more. Upstairs, in the anteroom of the synagogue, two men, whose names I didn't learn, were cutting sheets of plexiglass set upon saw horses. Every glass window in the community was in the process of being replaced.

Downstairs in the community lounge, 320 people came for lunch daily. Two-thirds were community members. Tzitzko prepared meals on one of three stoves set up behind a rigged curtain, one for gas, another for wood, a third for electricity. He prepared whatever he had, and what he had depended on the convoys allowed into the city and Nada's storeroom. Even in the best of times, the food was little more than filling. But Tzitzko never failed to don a white smock and ladled each helping out with one hand

elegantly behind his back. He served rice mixed with spinach, pasta and tinned fish, lentils with flecks of tinned meat or sometimes canned ravioli. Nearly everyone brought containers for supper.

Nearby were the administration offices. Vera Fischer was the treasurer. Her strongbox often overflowed with near-worthless Bosnian currency and far smaller amounts of dollars, Austrian schillings, and German marks. Vera, who was divorced, sent her daughter to Israel early in the war. Later she sold her apartment and everything in it, then because her dog had gone nearly crazy from the shelling, she had him put to sleep. Now she lived in a small flat close to the community. As she smoked a cigarette and chatted from behind her desk, she said, "step by step I've given up everything here. I have almost nothing left, but still I can't make that final move to leave the city I was born in. No home, no possessions, no children hold me here now, but something does. I only know this: when I leave, I will never, ever come back, and someday soon, I will go."

Atzo, a handsome Bosnian Serb with a wife and daughter in Sweden, sat in an office outside Ceresnjes's, where he typed letters, filed reports, fielded appointments and calls for Ceresnjes, Finci, and Nikolich. These three often met with visiting journalists, dignitaries, politicians, UN commanders. It was obvious that they worked hard to stay on the best of terms with everyone who could be of help. And they welcomed every new UN commander to their office with coffee and conversation.

The walls in Ceresnjes's office were covered with photographs of rabbis from times past, one of them Tzitzko's grandfather. High above was a faded, black and white official portrait of Tito, something not seen in Serbia and Croatia now. Watching me eye it, Ceresnjes said, "I never even considered taking it down. After all, there was peace during the 35 years he ran the country. Now look at us."

Around the corner, a barber had set up a chair. Three men were waiting. A dentist would visit tomorrow. Upstairs was David Kamhi's office, where he organized La Benevolencija's cultural events. A bald man with thick glasses and ubiquitous fur hat, Kamhi was busy that day at his other job: "renting" apartments of community members who had fled to homeless Bosnian refugees. "Of course the refugees have no money," said Kamhi, "but we interview them quite seriously, have them sign a contract anyway, and send someone by to look in once in a while to make sure everything's okay."

Near Kamhi's office was the womens' club, La Bohoreta, where a dozen women congregated each day to knit sweaters, file reports, and assemble food packages for the bedridden. Nearby was a small room where a half-dozen people sat waiting to be called into the radio room. One at a time, Vlado or Timur ushered them to a chair and handed over a microphone. Then, a La Benevolencija volunteer sitting in an office in the Jewish community center in Zagreb either handed the other microphone over to someone sitting there, or patched a telephone call through to Israel, France, Great Britain or elsewhere. In off-hours, Timur, Vlado, and their counterparts in Zagreb would transmit messages in and out of Sarajevo.

To one side of the radio room, in what had been a small store room, Slobodon, the computer operator, sat banging away at one of the two computers on his desk. A tangled nest of wires ran every which way between them and two printers. Below sat three car batteries that provided power when the electricity wasn't working, which was most of the time.

The office of the medical division was down the hall. Under the guidance of Dr Igor Gaon, La Benevolencija set up three pharmacies around Sarajevo and provided over 1,600,000 free medical presriptions, five each for every man, woman and child in the city.

The community center first-aid clinic had three doctors and three nurses. During the siege they saw 2,500 patients, made over 630 house calls, and arranged nearly 300 home hospitalizations. Early in the war, Gaon established a network between his medical warehouse and those of the city's hospitals, and he could often be seen rumaging through the bowels of Kosevo Hospital, chatting with colleagues, taking orders and trading off stock.

On the morning I visited the community first aid clinic, a lanky man in his thirties was lying fully clothed on the cot in the examining room and Jadranka was massaging his neck.

Reading a letter from a loved one abroad in the Sarajevo Jewish community center. December 1993.

"Feel better?" she asked him, then turned to say hello to me.

I asked her if I could meet the chief doctor of the clinic. The man on the bed stood up and held out his hand. "Srdjan Gornjakovich," he said, smiling. "It's a slow morning."

The night before, Gornjakovic had slept over at one of his patient's homes, an elderly Muslim woman who was sometimes so afraid she couldn't sleep and her blood pressure climbed dangerously high. This doctor's prescription: stay up all night and talk with her. At dawn he hurried across town, doused his face with water poured from a jug into the sink, and waited for the new day's patients.

Over the next few minutes, seven Sarajevans knocked on the door of the first aid station. One woman had a dog bite, not uncommon in a city where domestic pets are left to forage for themselves. A middle-aged man came with a wound on his leg; he had fallen down stairs running from a mortar attack and had to have a new bandage. A patient came to have his blood pressure checked, a woman came daily to have a festering wound cleaned, two children were brought in for flu vaccines.

By this time it was nearly 12:30. Lunch was served from 12:00 to 1:00 and the lounge was filled with people. Rachela Dzidic had just arrived. Jacob Finci and Ivan Ceresnjes were talking with a city policeman at another table but Ivan came over to introduce me to Dr Vilem Wagman, a crinkly 84-year-old who had been born in Poland.

By 1:30 the room began to empty. By 2:30 only a few souls were left. The shadows of naked trees behind the synagogue had stretched across the narrow Miljacka river in its concrete culvert and onto the battered, pock marked buildings across the street. By 3:00 it was nearly silent, and those who remained were playing chess, or solitaire, or had propped themselves up in a corner with a book.

By 3:30 PM the shadows had melted into gray and it was growing dark. People were now bundling up for the walk home and the casual, noisy atmosphere from earlier in the day had disappeared. Faces were drawn as they stepped into the street and I watched them move carefully but quickly over the ice.

Bojan and Igor had left; so had everyone in the medical office. Vlado, who slept at the community, still manned the crackling radio, and was reading off messages Sarajevans had dropped by during the day

to his Zagreb colleague. Novo was standing in the community lounge, hooking up the television set to the generator in the basement. "We show a video movie every day around this time. You want to stay and see it?" he asked me as I headed for the door.

"What is it?" I said.

"I'm not sure. Djuro hasn't brought it in yet. I just hope its not a war movie."

"Why not?"

He chuckled. "Too amateurish."

It was 4:00, almost dark, and I knew I had stayed too long. I was convinced there were 3 shifts of snipers who began their work at 8:00 AM, 4:00 PM and midnight, because these were the times they were at their friskiest. I crossed over the pedestrian bridge and hurried through the city, now nearly dark. Not a single street light, or any light for that matter, could be seen, just the black shadows of the dying city cast against the black canvas of the winter night. I used my flashlight only rarely, as others did, and made my way up Titova Street. I chose my path and gait by a rule I formulated earlier in the week: on streets where people walk, it's okay to walk. On streets where they run, that's where I run. And on streets where no one goes, don't go.

Still, surrounding the battered Holiday Inn, there was that stretch of no man's land – 200 yards of open space where the snipers in the Jewish cemetery on the hill had a clear shot and were said to use infrared night scopes. I ran across the ice as fast as I flat-footedly could, huffing along with my camera bag thudding against me until I reached the shadow of the hotel that blocked the view from the hill.

That night, there was neither electricity in the Holiday Inn, nor water. But the hotel staff cleaned the rooms, the restaurant was lit by a generator, and food was served in style by waiters in bow ties and green jackets. No one complained about the quality. To finish the evening, there was a local brandy-like substance touched only by the bravest. Someone dubbed it, rather dubiously, "ethnic cleanser."

My days in Sarajevo did not vary much. Friends and colleagues would leave the Holiday Inn each morning for UN press conferences, trips up to Pale to interview Bosnian Serb leaders, or to the Bosnian presidency. Other photograpers and reporters simply walked outside the Holiday Inn each morning, faced the day before them and headed this way or that, searching for a picture, an article.

Me, I did Jews. Most days Rashu fetched me after breakfast and only rarely did I have to make the morning heave across no man's land. At the community center, I wandered around meeting people. There were walks and chats with Ljerka Danon. "Now be careful here," scolded the gray haired woman as we approached a corner near her home. "There are snipers, so you run, but wait until I make it across." It was as if she were teaching a country bumpkin the ways of the big city. Then I watched in amazement as she tore across the street and out of harm's way, faster, I noted, than I could run.

Other times I walked home with Dr. Wagman and his wife. As she helped him negotiate the overturned cars and burnt out houses and debris, he would look around, say a few words, tell a joke, and keep on shuffling. Once he said, "You know, Serotta – and by the way, your name means orphan in Polish so I don't know how wise it is for you to be here – I think about leaving Sarajevo, but then I ask myself, where should I go? My family went up in the chimneys of Auschwitz, every single one of them. I have my wife, that's all. Should I go sit in some box in the Israeli desert, or stay among my books, my papers, my friends, and my memories?"

Another day, as we walked past the central market not long after it was hit by a mortar blast and four people died, he said, "I don't worry about mortars and snipers. I worry about the future, as strange as that might seem to you. I'm an old Jew, and I have come to know this: staying is better than going. If you go, you lose your chance to leave. Better to always have it like a ticket to be used, but only if you really, really need it."

I also spent long hours with Finci and Ceresjnes. One evening, sitting in the breadbox-sized flat Ceresnjes inhabited not far from the community, he leaned forward and asked me, "Do you know what we need most now – I mean besides the food and medicine and a truck to drive up from the coast with our goods? We need a partner Jewish community in the west, someone who will help us rebuild, provide a Hebrew teacher, rebuild the synagogue, fund the repair work on the shul.

"You might think I'm crazy but what I want to do is prepare this community so that if any Jewish family abroad wants to come home, we will have made it a real, functioning community again." He paused. A sniper was hitting a target a few streets away. "We owe it to the Jews here. I just don't want to give up on what we've built since 1945."

I asked, "What do you hear from people who left?"

He frowned. "At first, I got a great many letters, and nearly all of them were filled with thank you's for what we had done for them, for getting them out. They wanted to know about their apartments, about the community, about their friends. They told us that they missed us and they wanted to come back as soon as possible. Now we don't get many letters. And when we do, the last thing they speak about is coming back. But the ones who write, write us in their private moments, when they feel guilty about leaving, or when they think about the old times."

Ceresnjes chuckled. "Nostalgia. Didn't you know? It's the Balkan disease."

La Benevolencija volunteers include Timur, a 19 year old Muslim student and Ljerka Danon (below), a 66 Jewish pensioner. January 1994.

Although very few Jewish children remain in Sarajevo, festivals and holidays are observed, and children from the neighborhood are given candy and treated to a clown's performance. January 1994.

Messages taken by radio operators are written down and delivered to Sarajevans throughout the city. January 1994 (right).

The community's two way radio, donated by Joint, has made some 10,000 connections to the outside world during the siege. November 1993 (above and below).

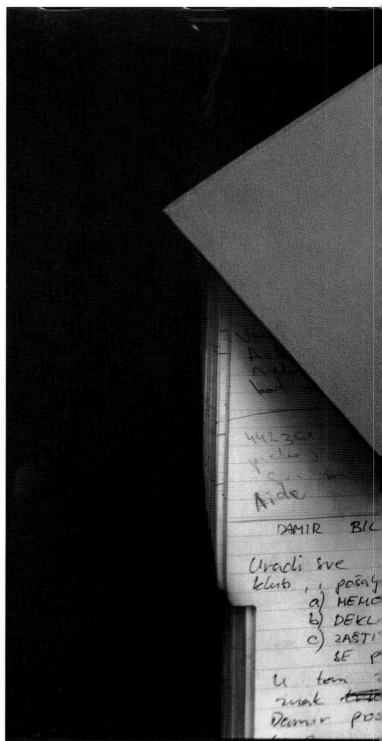

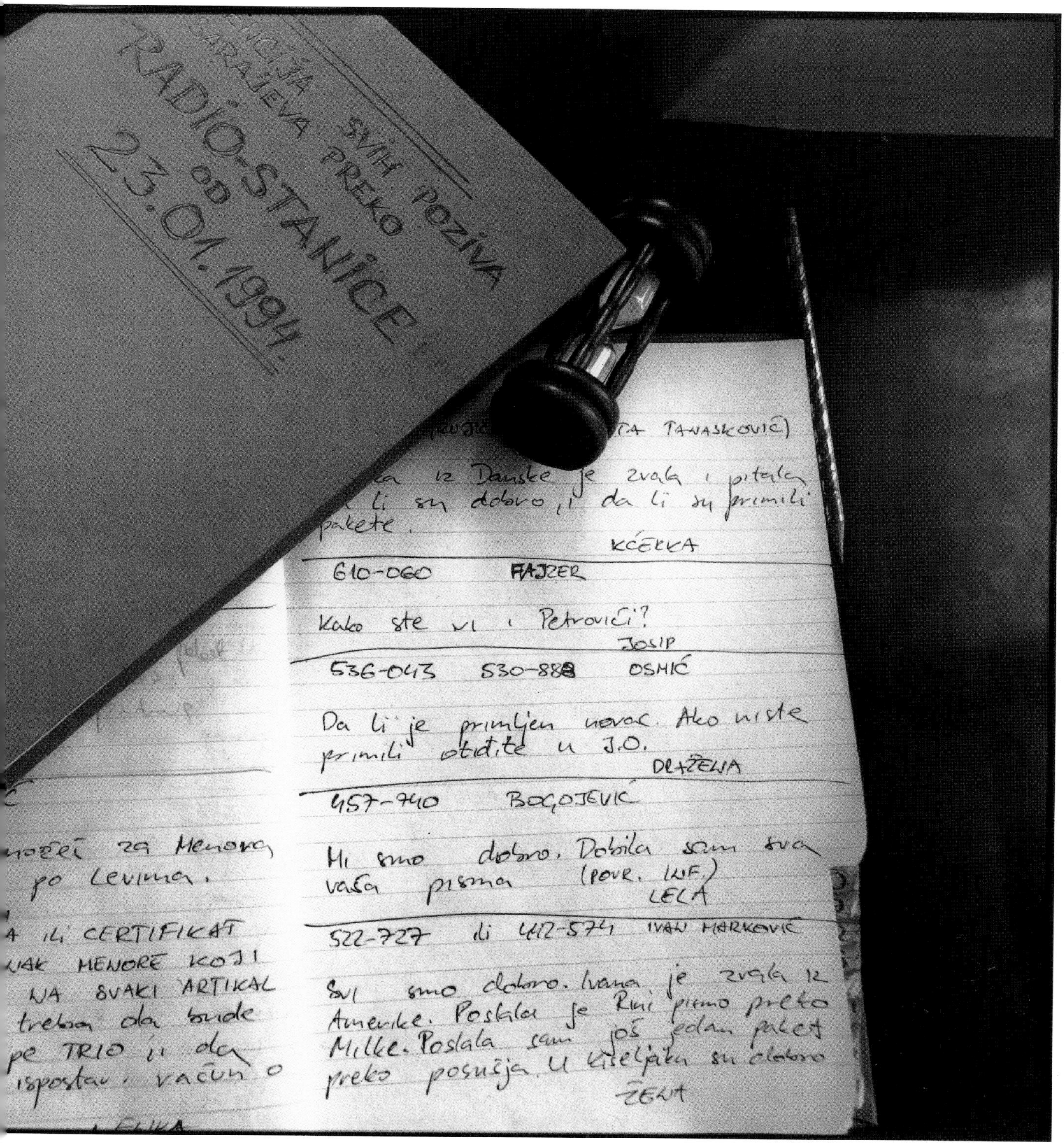

EVIDENCIJA SVIH POZIVA
SARAJEVA PREKO
RADIO-STANICE
OD
23.01.1994.

(RUJICA ... TA TANASKOVIĆ)

...a iz Danske je zvala i pitala
...li su dobro, i da li su primili
pakete.

KĆERKA

610-060   FAJZER

Kako ste vi i Petrovići?

JOSIP

536-043   530-888   OSMIĆ

Da li je primljen novac. Ako niste
primili otidite u J.O.

DRAŽENA

457-740   BOGOJEVIĆ

Mi smo dobro. Dobila sam sva
vaša pisma (POVR. INF.)

LELA

522-727   ili 412-574   IVAN MARKOVIĆ

Svi smo dobro. Ivana je zvala iz
Amerike. Poslala je Rini pismo preko
Milke. Poslala sam još jedan paket
preko poznieja. U Kiseljaku su dobro

ŽENA

...noseći za Menora...
po Levima.

...ili CERTIFIKAT
...AK MENORE KOJI
...NA SVAKI ARTIKAL
...treba da bude
pe TRIO ii da
ispostav. račun o

...ELIKA

63

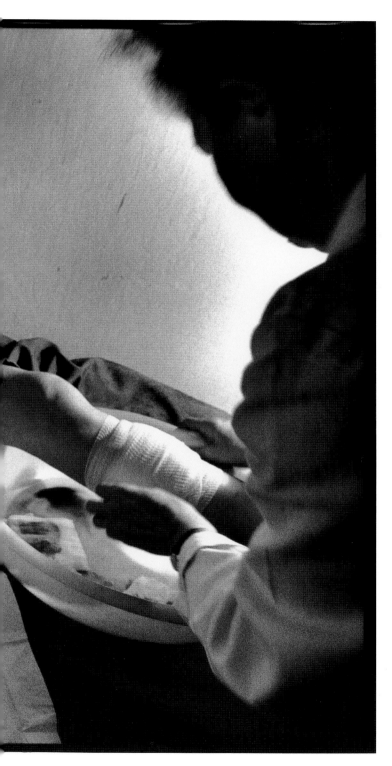

La Benevolencija has opened three pharmacies throughout the city and has distributed – without charge – 1,6 million prescriptions, many of which were donated by Doctors Without Borders (above).

La Benevolencija's first aid station has seen 2,500 patients and employs three doctors and three nurses, none of whom are Jewish. February 1994 (left).

Dr and Mrs Wilem Wagman heading home after fetching food supplies at the community center. January 1994 (above).

Vera Fischer, treasurer of the Sarajevo Jewish community, heading home on a January evening (right).

La Bohoreta, the Womens Club of the Jewish community, has been active during the war, by delivering food to the infirm, knitting and distributing clothes to Bosnian refugees, and preparing foods for Jewish festivals and holidays. Januray 1994.

71

House Calls

By the time I arrived in Sarajevo in November 1993, 10,000 people had been killed, including 2,400 children. Fifty thousand had been wounded, one out of every five Sarajevans. Not unwisely, people ventured out as little as possible. They knew which streets snipers had clear views of and made their way through the city via apartment hallways, back yards, through store fronts, then sprinted across streets where "Pazi!! Snaiper!!" banners hung. To block the killers' vision, doors, planks, stacks of containers, barriers of every sort were shanghaied into service. Some stretched across intersections, others ran like solid fences for several blocks.

Donka Nikolich in her Sarajevo apartment. December 1993.

Staying home could be just as dangerous as going out. One afternoon Rachela Dzidic was unlocking her apartment door when a mortar tore through the far wall, blowing a hole in her children's bedroom. She escaped unharmed. Others were far less lucky. A few blocks from the Jewish community center, the Dragnic family was just finishing lunch in early January 1994 when a mortar shell smashed into their apartment killing six people.

As dangerous as the city was, the Jewish community sent its doctors and nurses on house calls every week. One morning during my first visit, Srdjan Gornjakovich approached me in the community lounge where I was wrapping my hands around a warm coffee cup and asked if I felt like meeting one of his favorite patients. Slinging my camera bag over my shoulder, I followed him out the door, where Miki, a 44 year old Bosnian Serb nurse, was waiting.

It was snowing. The temperature hovered at 20 degrees Fahrenheit and the streets were iced over. Children were on their sleds, laughing as they played. Old people walked gingerly, muttering. They knew if they fell and hurt themselves, said Srdjan, they could be doomed. "Who would feed them, care for them if they were bedridden?"

We crossed Titova, lined with forlorn buildings pummeled by shells, its store fronts boarded over. We climbed upward. Offices and apartment blocks were left behind and now there were houses along winding alleys, each buttressed by a garden wall as high as the house itself. Behind these walls Sarajevans maintained their contact with God's world: plum and apple trees, rabbit hutches and chicken runs, row upon row of vegetables were grown here in summer, put into jars in autumn, and eaten in winter. These were the gardens that, when the siege came, staved off hunger and provided something to sell or trade in the central market.

In 20 minutes we reached a four-story apartment

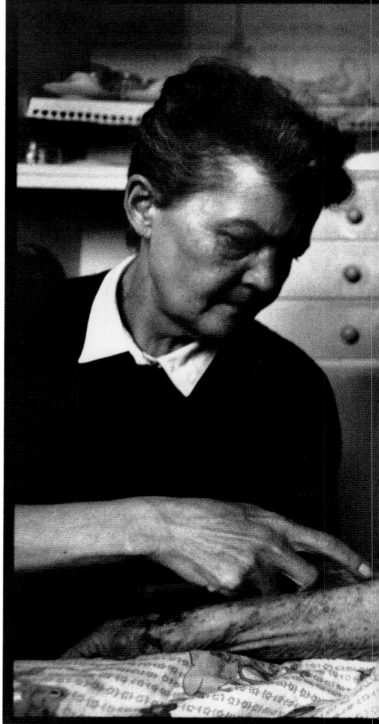

Miki, a Serb nurse working for the Jewish community, gives Mrs Nikolich an injection to help her breathe. December 1993.

74

house. We knocked on a door on the first landing. Eighty-four year old Donka-Zorka Nikolich answered. She was thin and frail and bundled in several sweaters, leggings and woolen knitted house shoes. She had pinned her mass of gray hair behind her in a bun and she let us in with a sigh as we followed her into the kitchen. She called over her shoulder in a raspy voice, "So sorry I'm alive to meet you. I feel horrible, Srdjan."

"This is Danilo Nikolich's mother," Srdjan said sotto voce. "She worries about him whenever he's *out* of Sarajevo – can you imagine? Anyway, she gets upset, her asthma gets bad, so we have to come see her."

Coats off, we gathered around her kitchen table. The room was painted blue. Souvenirs, calendars, and little paintings decorated the walls. Through the kitchen window a thin rubber gas line had been drawn from the street.

Srdjan Gornjakovich tends his patient Zeyneba Hardaga. November 1993.

It curled its way under the stove where it heated the oven and warmed the room. As the old woman handed Srdjan a coffee mill and beans to grind, she looked in the pantry for her plum brandy. "God how I wish I could die this morning," she grumbled. "I just hate winter afternoons." Placing the glasses on the table, she poured thimble-size glasses for Srdjan and me.

I watched with alarm as she climbed on a rickety stool to look for something in her pantry. Srdjan shook his head and lit a cigarette. "You can't stop her from climbing. She'll outlive us all, even though her heart is bad, her blood pressure high and she has chronic asthma, which isn't helped by the fact she smokes the roughest tobacco in the Balkans – which she rolls herself." She found what she was looking for: cookies.

After preparing coffee in a *dzezva*, a brass Turkish coffee pot, Donka Nikolich laid the cookies on a plate, sat down and offered me one. I declined, thinking of how few she must have. She shrugged, picked one up and carefully taking aim, shoved it

into my mouth as Srdjan collapsed in laughter. "See what I mean?"

A few minutes later, her sweaters were laid around her. Srdjan had warmed his stethoscope over the stove and he was now examining, listening to her tiny chest. Miki readied a huge syringe. Mrs. Nikolic was about to get an injection, one that would allow more air into her clogged lungs. The problem was finding a vein. After searching a minute or two, Miki slid the needle into a spot on her bony arm between the red splotches and bruises. The old woman gasped, her face contorting in pain. It would take Miki ten minutes and three attempts to complete the task.

In the meantime, Srdjan said, "most of my patients need one thing more than anything else: not to be alone. I can't tell you how many houses I sleep in just to keep someone company. Old people are often alone because many families have left. The old don't want to go and in the Jewish community, the old ones who have lived through Auschwitz or Terezin say to me, 'I've had it with being a refugee, of being forced out of my home. I'm not going anywhere.' And in truth, many are too old to travel and too scared. I don't even put them into hospitals if I can do everything at home."

Donka Nikolich's ordeal was over. The old woman sat quietly for a few minutes, gazing glassy-eyed into space. Then her eyelids fluttered and she hauled herself up and leaned over the table top. "Now where are my cigarettes?" she growled.

Srdjan and I headed outside and back to the community. Just at the entranceway, a strange whizzing sound tore through the air. Alarmed, I pulled back and asked, "Was that a bullet?"

Srdjan, who did not break his stride, said, "Yes, but don't worry, it was very far away."

Unsteadily, I followed and caught up with him. "That didn't *seem* very far away."

He smiled. "You wouldn't expect a doctor to tell the truth, would you?"

We walked on and I asked Srdjan about himself. He had been born in Zenica, he told me, the only child of parents who had him quite late in life. His mother was a Serb, his father a Vlach, a small minority in Serbia near the Romanian border. Both his parents were doctors. Srdjan studied at the university in Sarajevo and finished his residency a few months before the war. Trained as an emergency physician he went to Kosevo Hospital, Sarajevo's largest, but when he said he was a Serb, he was refused a job in his field. When he heard that the Jewish community was about to start its own clinic, Srdjan went to see Ivan Ceresnjes.

Zeyneba Hardaga's hands. November 1993.

"I sat down and Ivica said, 'First, can you do the job?' I said 'of course.' Next he said, 'Can we trust you?' I said 'of course.' He looked at me for a minute, then said, 'Okay. Go upstairs and go to work.'"

After that, Srdjan made hundreds of house calls and most of them to the elderly. Ceresnjes said that rarely has he seen such devotion by a physician, and even more rarely, how attached his patients were to him. Jacob Finci echoed this and said, "Sometimes we send by another doctor, and I'll get a phone call almost immediately from some old person. 'When is the doctor coming back to me?' But we sent you a doctor, I would tell them. They'd say, 'No, I mean the *real* doctor.'"

Srdjan said, "Maybe its because my own parents are old, and were old when I was growing up, that I have so much sympathy for people this age. The old ones have been through so much and it's awful for them to live their last years in this hell."

We had reached the footbridge across the Miljacka, and stood waiting for a convoy of UN armored personnel carriers to lumber by. From across the street on the other side, someone greeted Srdjan and asked how he was. Srdjan waved cheerfully and answered back something that made the man break out in a laugh. I asked what he said. "I always reply the same when people ask me 'how are things?'

'They'll get worse,' I tell them. And so far, I haven't been wrong."

Back at the community, over a lunch of pasta with tomato sauce and tinned fish, I asked Srdjan if there were maladies traceable directly to the war. "Sure," he said.

"Children suffer mostly from digestive problems. Stomach cramps caused from stress are common, as is diarrhea from the unclean water. It can be severe. Of course, psychologically, children cannot concentrate, they have become hard to discipline and there is much bed wetting. Nothing is sure in their lives, and that's bad for any child – knowing your father and mother are as powerless as kittens. I cannot imagine how bad all this will be on society a few years from now.

"In general, the middle generation suffers from active ulcers much more than in normal times. Chronic depression is not uncommon and they have the most number of suicides and total emotional breakdowns. They have seen their children killed or their friends. They have seen their entire life savings and possessions go up in smoke. Lawyers and university professors now sleep in borrowed flats, wear clothes donated to them and watch in the mirror as they get thinner and thinner. All adults here have lost, on average, 20 pounds. Teeth are going because of the diet. People lose or crack their finger nails, toe nails. Their hair falls out. Some people just break down.

"As for the old, they are afraid to go outside. They cannot lift the heavy water jugs up to their apartments and they become so weak from hunger and fear and loneliness they just wither away. High blood pressure and chronic heart problems are their worst enemies – and their most frequent visitors."

The next day Srdjan and I left the community and headed up Skenderija to meet Zeyneba Hardaga. Since the war began, her neighborhood had been over run by Bosnian Serbs and she was living with her daughter Aida, son-in-law Branumir Pecanac, and ten year old grand daughter Stela on the top floor of a seven-story high rise with no electricity or gas. Srdjan and I climbed the stairs. A busted skylight filtered soft gray light into the stairwell. Water from icicles plopped into puddles in the darkness below.

Branumir suffered from multiple sclerosis and this left Aida to fend for the family alone. Each day the former economist faced the seven flights with sacks of wood for the fire, food for the family and heavy jugs of water.

Stela jumped into Srdjan's arms as soon as we entered the apartment. Zeyneba Hardaga remained seated, wearing a flowing Muslim-style dress and headgear. She had clear gray eyes and tanned, leathery skin. Gnarled hands wrapped themselves around a wooden cane.

After introductions, Srdjan laid Zeyneba Hardaga out on the sofa she inhabited during the day, always in site of her Righteous Gentile Award. She looked over the certificate from Yad Vashem so many times its edges were frayed and brown, never mind that she could not read the English or Hebrew. She showed me her scrap book of her visit to Israel.

The woman's hands stroked Srdjan's blue-jeaned sleeve as he examined her. He nodded and told her she's doing a bit better. Then as he placed his equipment back in his bag, he said to me in English that her high blood pressure was getting worse and she suffered from chronic heart trouble. "If she stays in Sarajevo, she will die," he said.

Peering over my Leica, I asked if she could leave on one of the Jewish community's convoys.

"Ask Aida to tell you about it over lunch," he said.

"Yes, you're staying for lunch," said Aida, standing at the door.

"But I can't stay for lunch, I just ate," I said, lying, not wishing to gobble up their food.

"He's lying," said Srdjan flatly in English.

We sat down to a huge lunch of pasta with tomato sauce, a rice pilaf cooked with potatoes and a soup made with pasta and herbs. In the wood-fired oven, Aida was baking a bread cake, and on the stove top she had melted a chocolate bar to sprinkle over it when it was done.

Srdjan prodded Aida to tell me what had happened to the family. She reddened but said nothing. Srdjan shrugged and began on his own.

"Zeyneba was to have been on a convoy out of Sarajevo and brought to Israel. She has an invitation to live there as a guest of the government. But her name, for some reason, was removed from the list of those allowed to leave Bosnia. Worse, her family's name wasn't even on the list." He glanced down at Stela, who was sitting on his lap, cuddled against him. "And this too: the family is not invited to come to Israel at all."

"Some way to treat a hero," I said.

We ate on in silence. I asked if they had gone again to the authorities. They had tried everyone but to no avail. The Jewish community had been trying to help for more than a year.

Then Aida stood up and went to the window, partially covered with cardboard ever since a sniper shot it out. "We all want to go to Israel, its true," she said. "My mother talks about it all the time. She showed you this scrap book of her visit there in 1985. She fell in love with this country, and she's very attached to the family of Josef Kabilio." She raised her hands, then dropped them. "I just want to keep my family together," she said. "I'm asking for the smallest of chances."

Srdjan drubbed his fingers on the table. Then he looked at me and said, "Can you do anything?"

I shrugged. "Do? What can I do? I can write an article. I can call the president of Joint, Ambassador Wolf. But that's about all I can really do."

"But that would be nice. That would help," said Aida. "And we would be very grateful."

It was only then that I realized the whole visit had been a set-up: the lavish food, Zeyneba Hardaga's best clothes. I could not imagine why these people had invested so much in me. By then it was nearly dark and Srdjan said he would sleep over that night and that I should hurry back to the Holiday Inn.

I thanked everyone for the hospitality. I promised to do what I could. Stela led me down the silent staircase with a candle, all seven freezing stories, our shadows dancing off walls. It was snowing again, and the snow flakes swirled around the stairwell.

I turned out into the street and scurried toward the hotel, over the ice, past the destroyed buses, burnt-out, fish-nosed trams, and mangy dogs that roamed the streets of Sarajevo. The hotel had electricity that night and I sat on the floor next to my pint-sized electric heater. I stared at the computer screen for a while, then dashed off an article about Zeyneba Hardaga I hoped someone might take. Then I went to use BBC's satellite phone and called Joint's New York office. I told Milton Wolf who I had just seen. He knew all about the Hardaga case and was working on it. "It's funny," he said. "I just saw 'Schindler's List.' And I wonder if anyone has thought of the obvious. While it's nice to commemorate a hero, the problem is this one is alive, and the woman who would not abandon the Jews should not be expected to abandon her family. Not in Sarajevo."

The article I wrote that night was published in the Washington Post on 12 January as "A Hero Abandoned." I was told by Joint that 48 hours later, Zeyneba Hardaga and her family had their invitations for Israel, and the Bosnian government okayed their names for the next convoy list.

Srdjan took me on one more house call. Elias Danon, who had been having prostate problems, was in terrible pain. Ljerka Danon greeted us at the door. Her husband was lying on a red velvet sofa, blankets wrapped around him. Srdjan donned gloves and went to work tending his patient, with Jasna, a nurse, assisting. A minute later he said that it was time for surgery, and soon. How soon, Elias Danon asked. Srdjan looked at his watch and said we should take him to the French Hospital immediately. Jasna reached for the telephone.

Srdjan Gornjakovich and Stela, Zeyneba Hardaga's granddaughter. November 1993.

While Srdjan tended her husband, Ljerka Danon fetched an overnight bag and packed her husband's night clothes. Then she left the one heated room in the house and returned a minute later with a laden tray. "Surely an emergency call has enough time for coffee," she said as she laid out cake, plum brandy and cigarettes on the table, then took to grinding the coffee beans.

Srdjan smiled. "The hospital will be standing in another hour," he said. "Or most of it, anyway."

We drank our coffee and they smoked their cigarettes. Ljerka kissed her husband good-bye while Srdjan and Jasna helped him down the stairs. Rashu had already warmed up the car and we drove down through windy, switch backed streets and alleys to the entrance of the French Hospital.

Inside, Srdjan guided Elias into the admitting doctor's office where he was signed in and turned over to a nurse. We took the sole operating elevator to a wing where there was no running water or electricity. Only a tiny hiss of steam heat came from the radiator next to the bed. The nurses brought in fresh sheets, Jasna helped Elias into bed, and Srdjan said he'd come by tomorrow, before surgery.

"He'll be okay, if the shells don't get him. I think our surgeons are excellent and they've gotten better since the war. In Sarajevo orthopedists hold bones together with nuts and bolts from cars and radiologists use parts from television sets for their equipment. We've learned to be creative. We've had to." Jasna had gone on ahead to make another house call with Rashu, and as Srdjan and I left the hospital by the front door, a half dozen soldiers, one without a leg, another with a bandage over an eye, another couple with stumps for arms, made their way past us inside. Not far away we heard the throaty whoosh of a mortar shell tearing through the air. It crashed into a nearby building. In the distance came the crack of sniper fire.

Just then an ambulance was racing toward the hospital's emergency entrance and two doctors and a nurse ran past us. Outside, Srdjan leaned against a wall and took in the cold, sharp air. "You think you could help me find a way of getting out of this city?" he asked.

I shrugged. "I'll be happy to try. Give me your CV and all your papers. I'll send them to some well-connected people I know in the States, but I'm not very optimistic."

He chuckled. "Optimistic? Now what is an optimist in Sarajevo? For twenty-two months I've been walking these streets. I really love my patients but I don't know how much more of this I can take." He moved away from the wall and looked at me. "I'm thirty-one years old," he said. "I thought I was going to have a life. I am still young enough."

Later that night, the Bosnian Serbs tried to repeat

their success of the previous evening, when they sent a shell through a wall of the Kosevo Hospital, killing two nurses. This time the target was the French Hospital. As I wrote in my computer the notes from earlier in the day, shells thudded heavily into the earth, shaking the ground and rattling the plastic windows in my dark room. I blew out the candle, grabbed a flashlight and bundling up, took a camera downstairs. Hugging the side of the hotel, I watched as two more shells were launched at the hospital where Elias Danon was lying. They all missed that night and crashed their way into a couple of abandoned skyscrapers. You could hear the glass fall down several flights as the sound echoed out on the street they call Sniper Alley.

Srdjan visits Elias Danon in his room in the French Hospital. December 1993.

Exodus

Rachela Dzidic held the pen in her hand so tightly it almost snapped. Holding her breath, she signed her husband's name and hers to the list, then slid the paper back to Danilo Nikolich. Now she had done it. She had signed up, once again, to get out of Sarajevo on the next Jewish community rescue convoy. It was now November 1993 and she had not seen her two sons for nearly 20 months. Danilo Nikolich said they hoped the convoy would leave the second week of January.

She entered the lounge, where we sat and talked. "I cannot allow myself even a tiny bit of optimism," she said. "I cannot bring myself to pack, arrange anything, or even tell anyone. First, we don't

Jewish community leaders visiting Bosnian Prime Minister Haris Silajdzic in his Sarajevo office. January 1994.

know if the convoy itself can go. Then, I don't know if I can go on it."

Her worry was not misplaced. Since autumn 1992, only one Jewish community bus left Sarajevo. That was in August 1993, and it took only 24 elderly and infirm community members. Since then, matters between the warring factions had degenerated and plans for several other convoys, from the UN, Red Cross, and others, had to be scrapped. That November, however, the Jewish community sent out feelers to the Serbs, the Bosnian government and the Croats, asking about the possibility of sending a convoy through all their territories to the coastal town of Makarska on the Adriatic. They encountered no objections and began making preparations. People were told to get their papers in order.

In the first week in January, Joint specialists Eli Eliezri and Doron Tashtit flew into Sarajevo. Together with Finci and Nikolich, in an UNPROFOR armored personnel carrier, they crossed the airport tarmac where Serb gunners faced off Bosnian government forces. Past the front line, they drove down a mud-filled alley to the Bosnian Serb command center in Lukavica. Here they discussed possible routes with Serb military leaders and liaison officers. The Serbs listened. Questions were posed and answered. Over the next few weeks, Eliezri and community leaders would make their way to and from Lukavica several times. Finally the letter of permission came from the Bosnian Serb deputy chief of staff, Manojlo Milovanovic.

Because the bus convoy would have to travel through both Croatian-held parts of Bosnia as well as Croatia itself, Jasha Bienenfeld went to work in Zagreb, securing buses, fuel, and the official permissions the convoy would need. He decided to go with the convoy himself, into and out of Sarajevo.

The Bosnian government also had to be informed of every move. They controlled who would be able to leave – no man between 18 and 55 – and what they could take with them – no books, bed sheets, silver or dishes, electrical appliances, household gadgets, weapons.

As the weeks went by in January, Sarajevans came to the Jewish community, asking about the list, always the list. They asked to have their names added. The list grew. It climbed up to the 100 mark and shot past it to 150. It remained there for a few days then a rush of names brought it to 200. It grew still. Even late at night, when the city lay dead and pitch black, a single light on Dobrovoljacka Street could be seen as Danilo Nikolich sat with a battery driven lamp next to his desk, adding, subtracting, moving names from column to column, making the check marks, question marks, circles, and sometimes, sadly, X's.

Negotiations with Bosnian Serb military leaders in their headquarters in Lukavica. January 1994.

Eliezri was losing patience. The list had to be approved by the Bosnian Interior Ministry before transport could be arranged. Finally, during the last week of January, a preliminary list was sent to the Ministry and the Bosnian Army Command. They checked the names, looked them up on their files, and allowed or disallowed the exit visas. Nearly every name was approved.

Rachela Dzidic could not ask. She had gone too far the last time. But every day after work, which she finished at 11:30 AM, she walked that long and dangerous mile to the community center. There she sat in the lounge in a chair facing the office, and waited.

"I am paralyzed with worry," she said. "I wrote to some American friends and asked if they could do something, anything, to get us out of here. They wrote me a sympathetic letter, and I'm sure they are trying. But they ended by saying 'don't do anything foolish.'" She smiled. "Can you imagine? What could I do more foolish than stay here?"

From her purse, she produced a plastic envelope holding letters on pink writing paper and color snapshots. "These are from my sons. I carry them with me everywhere." A bronzed boy, twelvish, thin and handsome, was standing next to his chubbier, more cheerful looking younger brother.

Unfolding one of the letters, she read, "'Dearest Mom and Dad, I hope you two have enough to eat. We can't wait until we see you. Can you imagine not seeing your Mom and Dad for so long? It makes no sense!!! The pictures you saw of us last time were at a picnic, where all the Yugoslavs went. It was nice and we talked about the old times (I am becoming a philosopher!).

'From here in Israel we send you thousands of best regards and a million best wishes for your anniversary and birthday. Most of all your son loves you very, very, very much.'"

Rachela Dzidic had tears in her eyes, but she pulled out another letter, and without looking up, said, "This one is from my younger son, Denis.

"'I really hate to write but grandfather says you love to read so I'll write this. I can't wait to see you. We're okay here. If I need anything, they give it to me. We have an Israeli family who comes to take us to their house every two or three days. They are really nice. I am now used to being the smallest kid around. There is no snow in Jerusalem. Well there is but not much. I keep my locker clean and my room. You would be proud of me. Your dearest Denis loves you very much.'"

Rachela wiped back the tears. "So you see, I come here every day. Once in a while, I manage to make a telephone-radio link up with them from here in the community. This is wonderful, but it's so hard to make the connection. And when we do speak, it can be terrible. Denis asked me if we didn't love him anymore, and if we did, why hadn't we come yet.

Every one in his family made it out of Sarajevo except his mother and father." She sighed.

Eliezri was just stepping out of the office and motioned to me with his chin. Excusing myself, I headed toward the door. Rashu drove Eliezri, Finci, Ceresnjes and me into the center of town and to the rear entrance of the Bosnian Presidency, a massive, graying Austrian-era building that had taken relatively few hits from the surrounding hills.

We presented our credentials, walked a long carpeted hallway and into the office of Haris Silajdzic, Prime Minister of Bosnia, who greeted Ceresnjes and Finci by the diminutives friends use: Ivitca for Ivan, Jacitca for Jacob. Coffee was served and it was clear that the visit was primarily social.

Eli Eliezri, a special representative of Joint, sent to Sarajevo to help with the rescue convoy. January 1994.

After introductions and small talk, Eliezri asked the Prime Minister, "Where is your family?"

"Pakistan," came the reply.

"Why Pakistan?"

"Well, first, there aren't any Serbs there …"

Silajdzic asked about the convoy and the list. Ceresnjes said nearly everything was okay, but one name had been removed from the list by the Interior Ministry. He said, "This is a woman, not some able-bodied soldier, and she has two sons in Israel who she hasn't seen in almost two years."

The Prime Minister's brows darkened and he reached for his pen. "Give me the name," he said. "I can't imagine why they would want to keep someone like that."

I felt a lump in my throat.

"Rachela Dzidic," said Ceresnjes.

"Get me her papers and numbers. Give them to my assistant." He walked over to his desk and pushed a button on his telephone. "Ivitca, you be sure and phone us this morning." Then he sat back down and raised his coffee cup. "I wouldn't worry."

Ceresnjes sighed, "Unfortunately, Mr Prime Minister, this is what we were told when her name was removed last time."

Silajdzic smiled. "Ah, but you didn't tell me, now did you?"

I returned to the community with Ceresnjes and Finci. Eliezri left for the airport and the next aid plane out to Zagreb. Rachela Dzidic was still sitting in the same chair and she was still staring at the office door. Ceresnjes saw her out of the corner of his eye. He stepped into the office and up to the desk. He took a pencil and piece of paper, scribbled a note and pulled the Prime Minister's assistant's card out of his jacket and laid it before his secretary. He walked up to Rachela Dzidic and me, and said cheerfully, "Come on, I'm buying you both lunch today. The chef is a personal friend of mine."

Eliezri called on the two way radio the next morning from Zagreb. He was bringing the buses into Sarajevo at dawn on Saturday morning, 5 February. He said Finci should spread the word, especially to the Bosnian government: the Jewish convoy was coming in, and it was going out on that date. Eliezri would tell the press.

Finci, Danilo, and others manned the phones and sent out word. Then the Bosnian customs officials were called.

The next day a half-dozen young men wearing suits and carrying briefcases bulging with papers stepped into the community center and set up shop upstairs in the entranceway to the synagogue.

All during the following week, 294 Sarajevans packed their bags. Rachela Dzidic, who still had no idea her name, and fate, were being bounced around from office to office, said, "I think I can finally allow myself to get excited. I mean, there really is so much to do." Then she caught herself. "But I'll believe it when I am on the bus, and the bus is outside of Sarajevo. Not before."

Rashu, the community driver, who had also been granted permission to join his family, went home to pack his bags. I accompanied him to his flat, and by the light of a couple of candles, he brought out two suitcases from a closet. He packed mostly clothes for

his wife and children. Rummaging through a box, he pulled out photographs, color snapshots from his college days. "See this guy here? He was our teacher. He's now a big shot, a real Serb nationalist. When I knew him, I didn't even know he was a Serb."

There were pictures of his vacation cottage. "It was so wonderful, knowing you had your own private little house sitting high up in the cool mountains. We went often, winter and summer. Now, well, it's all gone. Burnt to the ground." He closed the suitcases. "I cannot tell you how strange this feels. I'm packing for a trip. I'm leaving my apartment. And all around me is our furniture, television set, the video, stereo, the children's toys, the cooking tools, all the things of a family living a normal life in a normal European city. But I am not taking a trip. I'm on my way to being a refugee: me, a college graduate electronics engineer. Most times, I can't believe it."

They came with suitcases on children's wagons. They came with duffel bags slung over their shoulders. They came with cardboard boxes on luggage carts, and they came with what they could carry by hand, by wheel, in cars, and in trucks. The Jews were bringing their suitcases to the synagogue. True enough, only 116 of the 294 souls on the list were Jewish community members, but I was struck as I watched a man drag his suitcases up the steps to the customs officials. After the inspection in the foyer, he donned a skull cap before taking the bags into the synagogue.

The hard winter light that morning washed across the wooden floor and the six pointed star in the window behind him seemed to glow a hot white. It was a sad and timeless sight. I remember as a child our Passover seders in Savannah, Georgia in the 1950s. My great uncle, bespectacled, graying, wearing a cream-colored linen suit, would read from the Hagaddah in Hebrew and English the story of the Exodus from Egypt. "And you shall tell this story to your sons, as if you yourself had come out of the land of Bondage." The Jew has been telling this story to his son for generations and centuries. And in every century, he has been expelled from his home, and sent on his way, carrying little else with him but his sacred books and the long collective memory of the Jew.

In this same Sarajevo synagogue, Jews came in the spring and summer of 1941, never to return home. But back then they were forced to come at gun point. Now, on that cold, sharp morning in February 1994, I watched as another Jew came to the *shul* with his suitcases and prepared to leave another European city. The difference this time was obvious, but still painful. These Jews did not want to leave, and their neighbors did not want them to go. They had integrated into this city and its society. And although their numbers were terribly diminished after the Holocaust, those few remaining had rebuilt their lives and their community and they could be proud indeed of what they had accomplished. But now, again, they were leaving.

"When the Jews are leaving it is a bad sign for the city."

Before dawn on Saturday morning, six buses, three luggage trucks and one fuel truck, dusty and splattered with mud from the long journey, drove through the silent, dying city of Sarajevo. Under the direction of Jasha Bienenfeld they parked in single file down Dobrovoljacka Street. It was quiet and the Bosnian Serbs were holding to their promise not to shell the city during the evacuation.

Everyone leaving on the convoy had crowded inside the community center. Family members and friends gathered on the sidewalk and the street. By 9:00 AM, the first bus coughed to life and crept up to the community's doorway. Inside Bosnian customs officers called out the names of the elderly and infirm who were to go on the first bus. The first name called was Zeyneba Hardaga. She and her family were body-searched, then they boarded. Dr Srdjan Gornjakovich came with them. The Interior Ministry had allowed him to travel with the convoy under the condition he would return to Sarajevo. He promised he would.

Slowly, slowly, 294 people went through this process. The old, the young, Muslims, Jews, Serbs and Croats. There were but two steps onto the bus, and as each Sarajevan found a seat, a cry of recognition went up outside, hands touched the glass on both sides, and tears flowed. With unfathomable sadness in their eyes, family members and friends stood on the sidewalk and watched.

Rachela Dzidic held her husband's arm. She did not know that her name had been reinstated only hours before departure. She waved good-bye. "I can't believe it," she kept whispering, "I just can't believe it."

Community members' luggage awaiting the convoy. January 1994.

By early afternoon, the first three buses lumbered away. They had barely begun to move when a single 120 mm mortar shell roared overhead and crashed into the tin roofs of the central market stalls a kilometer away. It exploded with such force that bodies were blown completely apart. Sixty-eight dead were eventually identified. 200 people were wounded.

But no one on the buses knew this just then. Led by a procession of UNPROFOR armored vehicles, the buses rode through town, out into the suburbs, through that slice of Bosnian-Serb held territory near the airport, and finally onto the airport tarmac itself. There the convoy halted, and one bus driver at a time positioned himself between two white UN APCs. For half-a-minute they gunned their motors, and at a signal, all three tore off as fast as they could across the runway, where Bosnian Serb and Bosnian government guns faced each other on opposite sides. Sarajevans gripped their seats and held each others hands until the bus reached the end of the runway and the final UN checkpoint. The two APCs peeled off in opposite directions, roaring back across the tarmac to bring the next bus across the front line. All made the journey safely.

By nightfall, Dobrovoljacka Street was empty. Bojan, Igor, Atzo, Slobodon, Vlado, Novo and Timur lay limp and exhausted across the sofas in the community lounge. They had spent the past three hours loading the luggage, nearly six hundred pieces, and all by hand. Nearby Tzitzko cooked up a special dinner of grilled meats served with cold beer. They listened to the radio reports from Kosevo Hospital about the market place massacre.

The buses drove into Serb territory for half an hour and came to a halt on a road pocketed in a narrow river valley. Here the convoy was to meet its

89

As Rachela Dzidic (below) and 293 other Sarajevans say goodbye to the city, family members bid an emotional farewell, then head for home, alone. February 1994.

armed Serb escort, but it was nowhere to be seen. Jasha Bienenfeld, who had been tense ever since the mortar attack, drove off to the Lukovice barracks to talk with the Bosnian Serb command. Eliezri remained with the convoy.

Night fell. The hours went by and I walked the length of the convoy with Rachela Dzidic and her husband. Zeyneba Hardaga's grand daughter Stela ran past with other children. No one had any idea why Bienenfeld was taking so long. We had arrived at 5:00 PM, and now it was nearly 9:00 PM. Eliezri waved away questions with a smile. "Everything is under control. Nothing to worry about, *No-thing!*"

He was chain smoking and pacing. "Is everything okay?" I asked.

"Is everything okay?" he asked me back. "This is the middle of nowhere. This is the middle of a war. There has just been a horrible massacre. Jasha Bienenfeld alone holds the key for us to enter Croatian territory. Jasha has been gone for nearly four hours. Now *you* ask me if everything is okay? Sure. Everything is just fine," then he walked out of the red arc of the fuel truck's tail lights, and into the darkness.

Just after 10:00 PM two Volkswagen Golfs came flying out of the night and whisked past the buses. As they went Jasha Bienenfeld, riding in the passenger seat of the first car, leaned halfway out and bellowed for everyone to get in the buses – and fast. The second car had our Bosnian Serb military escort. People scurried about, the engines rumbled to life, the doors of the six buses hissed shut. We drove off into the long Balkan night.

Within minutes the ground rose. We drove on narrow highways huddled alongside river valleys, then zig-zagged over icy mountains. Through the headlights I could see a road covered with snow and alongside, a sheer drop down the cliffs.

We stopped at checkpoints in Trnovo and Dobro Polje. We turned south before Brod. Past midnight, people peaked out to watch as the convoy crept along. Some houses we passed lay destroyed, mosques had been blown up and bulldozed away. We followed the black flowing waters of the Piva River and left it to trace one of its tributaries through Tjentiste, Suha, and Grab, stopping for Bosnian Serb checkpoints in each.

South of Grab the road climbed steeply on switchbacks carved into the rock face. The fuel truck, which was leading the convoy, could not cope with the ice, and for nearly an hour sand and dirt were thrown down on the roadbed before it. Each bus, with only inches to spare, crept around the hapless truck, and left it, temporarily, behind.

Riding sometimes in the last bus, and viewing the convoy as it lumbered through snow-covered, alpine valleys, I shuddered to think of how frail it all looked: 294 suddenly stateless souls in 6 dinky buses, 3 rickety luggage trucks and one grunting fuel truck, making our way through a rock encrusted landscape where icicles hung like fangs in mountain passes.

After Grab, the road leveled off at 3,600 feet. The terrain was a muted blue-gray: snow under a weak moonlight. The mountain top town of Cemerno, sitting on the edge of the world, stared out over the entrance way into Hercegovina. We followed the road, little more than a dirt, ice-slick trail, steeply downward into Gacko. Then we climbed onto a badly-paved road that arched over the Dabarsko Polje mountain.

Here was the heart of the karst, that vast, lifeless range of limestone outcrop that stretched over much of the south Slav lands. Here the anemic soil produced little more than stone, heartbreak, and poverty. I could not imagine anyone fighting over it. The road followed the ridgeback high above the valleys on either side. We drove downward and caught up with a narrow river gorge. Dawn finally slid over the mountains around us just as we reached the last checkpoint of Bosnian Serb territory.

It took the better part of an hour for Bienenfeld to clear permission with the men in uniform sitting in the hut.

We had been expected. We were late. They lifted the bar guarding the road and we drove into another no-man's land. As we rounded a curve, we saw in the distance a bevy of uniformed men. Between them and us the road was covered with land mines.

The buses stopped. No one got out save Bienenfeld, who took the letter Eliezri provided from the president of Hercog-Bosna, the Croat-declared autonomous region of Bosnia. The soldiers slowly and carefully cleared the mines. We entered the historic border of Croatia at Metkovic, a city wrecked and ruined from the battles of autumn 1991. Picking up speed, the buses sailed down the highway, escorted now by blue and white Croatian police cars. At Ploce we could see the coast, and then we were on it: the vast spectacle of harsh mountains crashing directly into the turquoise Adriatic and across the sound, the long, narrow Peljesac peninsula. Sunshine cracked through the haze. It was a fine Mediterranean day. Now out of harm's way, people began falling off to sleep as the buses, cruising at speed, undulated softly. The smell of salt air wafted in through the half-open skylights.

That evening, if passing travelers happened to step into the Hotel Biokovka in Makarska, they might wonder why it was the handsomely dressed Rachela and Atif Dzidic were standing in the telephone booth, alternating between laughing and sobbing as they passed the telephone between them. They might wonder as well who the elderly Muslim woman was on the hotel's terrace, surrounded by reporters like a movie star holding court. And they might wonder whose children these were running along the beach, laughing, skipping stones and playing with wild abandon, acting as if they were seeing the ocean for the first time.

If those same travelers walked into the center of town, with its bright lights and shops and restaurants and outdoor cafés, they would come across couples they might mistake for tourists; people wearing sport coats and ties, fine dresses and high heels. If they stopped to listen, they would hear, however, that they were speaking neither Serbian nor Croatian, but that Bosnian dialect between the two, and some would know that these were Sarajevans.

I walked the town that evening, and people smiled and came up to me, but it took a moment or two to realize with whom I was speaking. Oh you look so nice, I would say, surprised, impressed, embarrassed. I didn't recognize them now that they looked like middle-class Europeans once more. You look so – so – different. Then they walked off, arm-in-arm, to goggle at the shop windows, and stroll by the harborside as the city lights behind them wiggled in the quayside waters.

Over the mountains above Makarska, up the Neretva River valley and over Mount Igman, Sarajevo lay prostrate, and in darkness. The massacre of the previous day would quickly bring about western sabre-rattling. The shelling of the city would stop. A Federation of sorts would be signed into being between Croats and Muslims, but few would believe this would last. The war would go on.

That Sunday, 6 February, the Jewish community of Sarajevo was 116 members smaller than it had been the previous day. But Moris Albahari still came to lunch at noon, and so did the Danons, and so did old Dr Wagman. Ceresnjes, Finci, and Nikolich said they would be leaving Sarajevo to join their families in Israel sometime soon, but then, they had been saying that for the past 22 months. In the community center they would be joined later by Srdjan Gornjakovich, who returned to tend his patients. "I still want out," he told me in Makarska. "But some of my patients still need me, and I can't leave them. Not yet."

Srdjan tended his patients, Tzitzko donned his white apron, Bojan and Igor delivered the post, Nada handed out food, Vlado and Timur sat at the radio, and Vera counted the money. Together, under the guidance of Finci, Ceresnjes, Nikolich, and friends from abroad, Sarajevo's Jews continued teaching their friends and neighbors the painful, bitter lesson Jews have been learning for centuries: how to survive.

The six buses make their way across the airport Tarmac and through the last UN checkpoint before heading into Bosnian Serb territory. February 1994.

Joint president and former US Ambassador Milton Wolf greeting Zeyneba Hardaga at the Croatian coast. February 1994.

Zeyneba Hardaga watching Bosnia slip past. February 1994.

97

Learning to Fly

If the boy had not lived a life filled with uncertainty and rootlessness, he would not have reached out to me. And if I, alone in my mid 40s, had not left behind a trail of broken relationships and a failed, childless marriage, I would not have been so willing to receive him. But during the course of making this book in Sarajevo and Jerusalem, Denis Karalich,

Denis and Radoslav on New Years Day, 1994.

searching for a heart, found a hole in mine, and climbed in.

He came from a broken home. His Bosnian Muslim father, Haris, had met a Polish Catholic woman in Germany and Denis was born in Munich in 1980. After an acrimonious divorce in 1988, the father returned to Bosnia, taking along his 12 year old son Jugopol and 8 year old Denis. He said the mother wanted nothing more to do with her sons. Haris Karalich secured work as a roofing contractor, first in Novi Travnik, then Donji Vakov. In 1991 the father and his two sons moved to Sarajevo and rented a room from Nada Levy, who worked at the Jewish community. Soon after, Jugopol left for Germany.

Denis Karalich became used to fending for himself. Moving from country to country and town to town, schools and friends drifted past him. He kept his emotions inside, but reached out to people, trying as best he could to find stability in his ever-changing world. When Nada Levy introduced Denis to her grandson Radoslav Bozovich, the two boys quickly became friends.

Before the war, they rode their bicycles out to the swimming pools of the city, laden with sweets and sandwiches they bought in the central market, or hiked together in the mountains surrounding Sarajevo. They played computer games and watched television together.

When war broke out, walks in the surrounding hills were impossible, and with no electricity the computer and television set stood idle. Haris Karalich found himself busier than ever with jobs from various aid agencies, and Denis, with his school now closed, often drifted through the ruined city alone. Radoslav too felt the isolation and alienation war brings. "All my old friends left Sarajevo, and the other children started calling me names, dirty Serb, dirty *Chetnik*, all because my mother's Serb and my dad half-Serb. Even a real good friend of mine, a Muslim boy, won't speak to me anymore. Only Deny doesn't call me names," he said.

"Well I don't care who's a Muslim, a Serb, a Croat," Denis muttered. "People who care about such things are sick." The boys grew closer together than ever.

With no school to take up their days, Nada began bringing the boys to the Jewish community center, a 30 minute walk through the besieged town. They helped Nada and Djuro Bozovich, Radoslav's father, who suffered from a deteriorating heart condition, in the food distribution center. They ran errands for him, prepared food packages for Nada, and in time became fixtures in the two-story building. They cheerfully helped Bojan and Igor sort the mail, offered to carry water for Srdjan up to the medical office, dragged cartons of food into Tzitzko's kitchen. Radoslav and Denis acted as the community center's unofficial greeters, and welcomed all visiting journalists.

During my visits, they traipsed along behind me. Radoslav, with bristle-topped brown hair and piercing eyes under heavily-lidded brows, asked dozens of questions about my cameras. Denis, tall, thin, and toothy, gave me advice on who to photograph. We sat and talked together every day. I conversed with Radoslav in English, which he had taught himself by watching television. Denis and I spoke in German. He had forgotten much and I had learned little, but it was enough to cement a bond.

On a cold January day, Radoslav plays with his gameboy in a sleeping bag at the Jewish community center.

On 5 January 1994, while Denis and Radoslav were alone at home, a mortar shell crashed into a house nearby. Radoslav lunged for the basement shelter and escaped unharmed. Denis ran for the window. Maybe someone's hurt, he thought. A second mortar exploded just at the base of their house. The concussion blew out the window and the force sent Denis – all eighty pounds – halfway across the room. The wall behind him was splattered with shards of glass turned into razor-sharp buckshot.

Stunned and in shock, the boy dragged himself up and lurched into the basement, blood dripping from his hand and shoulder. A shaft of glass was sticking out of his sweater and he jerked it out. "A woman who lives upstairs came running in," Denis said later when we met. "She fixed the wound on my hand; it was not so bad. But I wouldn't tell her about my shoulder because I thought a piece of bomb was stuck in me. I told her everything was fine and she left. I ran for the phone and called Rashu at the community and he came and got me. I only wanted Srdjan to look at me, because he'd know what to do."

Later that week, Ivan Ceresnjes spoke with Rado-slav's father Djuro Bozovich. It was a quiet morning. There was little shelling. Djuro Bozovich's heart was getting worse, and Srdjan Gornjakovic said if Djuro remained in Sarajevo, and if winter got much colder, he feared he would die. Ivan started to tell him of the next convoy but Djuro Bozovich cut him off. He could not entertain thoughts of his own exit, at least not yet. But as for his wife Natalia and son, for the first time he asked questions about Israel.

Natalia was 100 % Bosnian Serb, her parents were old and not well, and she had cousins and siblings in Sarajevo. But the attack on Nada's house, Radoslav's escape and Denis's injuries, settled the question for her. She went to Haris Karalich and said she wanted to take both Radoslav and his son to safety, and that meant to Israel.

It did not take much convincing for Denis. He had been badly shaken by that mortar attack. Radoslav wanted out as well. He kept having the same nightmare. He and Denis were dressed as soldiers and were walking the streets of Sarajevo machine-gunning everyone in their path. People screamed, guns belched, blood flowed. He woke up crying in the darkness of his ice cold room, and the nightmare returned time and time again.

From the moment their names were put on the convoy list, the boys spent their evenings in Denis's room huddled in their sleeping bags discussing what they'd do in Israel. Denis said, "We want to get jobs selling newspapers or something like that. We think it's best if we get bikes so we can go around and sell things in more places. Then we'll buy food and presents and give some of them to Natalia and we'll send the rest to Nada and Haris in Sarajevo."

Radoslav and Denis packed their belongings and stuffed them into plastic duffels. Natalia and Nada produced a new set of (second hand) clothes: brown leather jackets, turtle necks, colorful sweaters. Their friends came by on Friday, 4 February, the day before the convoy was set to leave, and sat around recording a cassette tape of messages for Denis and Radoslav to listen to in their new country.

100

By the time the sun set, Denis, who had been quiet and moody all day, quietly began to cry. His father tried to cheer him up but this only made matters worse. During the war, Haris Karalich, like nearly all able-bodied men, would not be allowed out of Sarajevo by the government. But he had said nothing about coming to Israel later and evaded his son's entreaties when he tried to pin him down.

Denis fell asleep with tears streaming down his face. They started anew the next morning. When it was time to leave the house, he held tightly onto his father's hand. He did not let go until Haris Karalich pulled it away inside the community center so he could ask about the buses. Denis crumbled and sobbed. Radoslav and Natalia sat on either side of him. "I'll be a good mother to you, Denis, I promise," Natalia said.

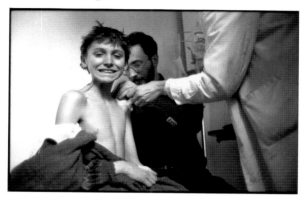

Denis, slightly wounded, is tended by Dr Srdjan Gornjakovich. January 1994.

It took more than an hour for Denis's name to be called. The police looked through his knap sack and asked if he was stealing any gold or hiding anti-tank mines. This made him smile, which lasted until he walked through the door, stepped twice onto the pavement, and into the bus. Just outside the window stood his father, who pressed his hands against the glass. Denis did the same and the tears began again. The boy who had not seen his mother for six years, and his brother for two years, was now bidding good-bye to his father. At the age of 13, Denis Karalich was being taken to his third country to learn his third language. As the bus drove out of Sarajevo and across the front line, all he was taking with him was Natalia's smile and the friendship of Radoslav.

By midnight, nearly everyone on the bus was asleep, but Denis stayed awake, watching Bosnia slip by in the darkness. We sat together in the back and I handed him my Walkman and some tapes. He listened to the Lemonheads for a while, then settled into Tom Petty. He played one song over and over,

and around 4:00 am, he asked what it was. He placed the earphones on my head. I smiled. "Ich lerne zu fliegen," I told him, "'Learning to fly.'"

He took the earphones back, rewound the song to its beginning and started it yet again. Over the rumble of the motor, he leaned against me, and while strumming his imaginary guitar, he sang sweetly, uncomprehendingly:

"Well I started out down a dirty road
Started out all alone

And the sun went down, as
I crossed the hill
And the town lit up, the world got still
I'm learning to fly
But ain't got wings
Coming down is the hardest thing"[1]

He sang on while I rubbed the top of his head. In the darkness, he couldn't see my eyes well with tears. Just after 10:30 on Sunday morning the doors of the bus opened in front of the Biokovka Hotel in Makarska. Radoslav, Natalia, and Denis dragged their bags up to the Jewish Agency desk. An Israeli representative listened to their story, rolled his eyes and took them to Tuvya Raviv, the tireless traveler who was helping everyone he could come to Israel. Raviv scanned the papers and said to me, "Am I to understand that this boy has no adoption papers from Mrs Bozovich? And she wants to bring him to Israel unattended by his parents?" He scratched his head and shook it from side to side. "And Denis, you're Muslim, right?"

"I'm nothing," Denis said. "I'm a human."

"My, my," Tuvya said and turned back to me. "This *is* interesting." He stole a look at Denis and Radoslav, both holding on to Natalia's hands.

"We'll just go to Serbia, or someplace else if Denis can't come with us!" Radoslav said.

Natalia nodded her head vigorously. "I'm a good mother to Radoslav. I'll be a good mother to Denis. But we have to stay together." Her lip was trembling.

Raviv sighed, waved his hand around and in a tired voice, said "Nema problema." Next to a blank

Radoslav in the Jewish community lounge. November 1993.

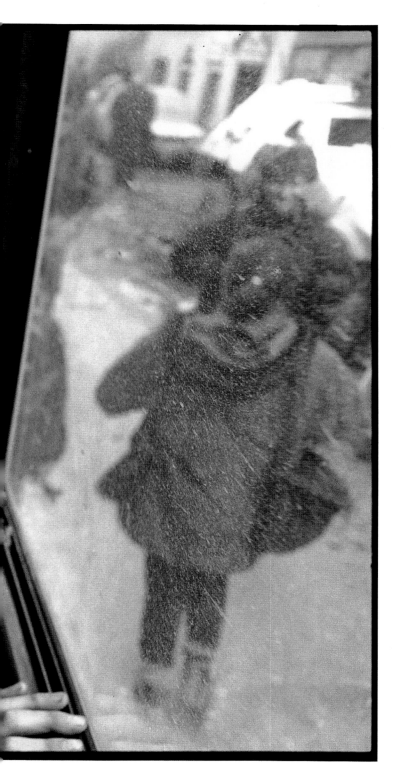

Radoslav asleep as the convoy makes its way through Croat-held Bosnia (above).

Denis bids a tearful farewell to Sarajevo, his father and his friends (left).

Denis on his first day of freedom. February 1994.

107

spot near Denis's name, he said to me quietly as he wrote, "It was, I believe, a Jewish grandmother the boy had, right?"

* * *

It was a mild April evening and the sound of jets screaming on the runway died away as I drove my rental car away from Ben Gurion airport and swung onto the highway toward Jerusalem. A half-hour later I followed the exit signs for Mevezerret Ziyyon Absorption Center. Stopping the first people I met on the street, I asked if they knew where the Bozovich family lived. They laughed. Twenty-five thousand people live here! Do you have a street, an address, anything? No? Then come back tomorrow when the office is open.

I drove further into the center, turning this way and that, past cookie-cutter, one and two storied flats and houses surrounded by scrub and eucalyptus. I said to myself, this is rather silly, so I stopped the car and climbed out to look around. To my right was a block of light in a doorway. Inside that light, I imagined the silhouette I was seeing was Denis. Fat chance, I thought. The silhouette started to move a bit, then it was running at full-speed toward me, and I heard a voice I knew well. "Du bist gekommen!" and in another second, he was jumping through the air as he flew into my arms. A moment after that, Radoslav was nuzzled against me, and Natalia stood nearby, hands on hips, shaking her head and laughing.

I stayed 10 days. We went to the beach in Jaffa and the Hard Rock Café in Tel Aviv. We walked the pedestrian streets of Jerusalem and swam in the pool at the American Colony Hotel. Both boys had fun, but in private moments, as Denis and I drew closer, I saw what the years of uncertainty and rootlessness had done to him. He worried when I got a parking ticket and asked four times in two days if I had paid it. He worried when I took him to lunch that he might be late for afternoon Hebrew class and secretly spied his watch every few minutes. He worried that he wasn't allowed to swim at the American Colony pool after dark, and I had to ask a waiter to come over and tell Denis, that as the chief manager of the hotel, he was giving him special permission. Saddest of all, while driving him from home from school one day, he asked, "When are you leaving Israel?"

"As I told you, next week."

"You're lying, you're lying! I see what you've done! You filled up the car with gas and you're taking it to the airport tomorrow and you're flying away, aren't you? Admit it!"

I looked over at him staring wide-eyed back at me. I thought, I should just gather him in my arms, hug him and tell him that I'll be the first adult who won't desert him. But that simply couldn't be true.

During that April visit, I asked, "Are you happy here in Israel?"

"No," came the speedy reply.

"What do you mean, no? You seem so happy and you have so many friends here now, don't you?"

"Friends have nothing to do with it! Nothing at all. Look, the Jews have their country, the Serbs have theirs, the Muslims theirs, the Croats theirs. All I know is that I was born in Germany and that's where I belong. That's where I want to go – where I must go – and they have to take me."

"When we're young, we talk in absolutes, Denis. But give it time. No country can be home before you speak its language. See how things are later."

"But I don't want to be here later," he said looking down at the floor.

"Well wait anyway. Study hard. Even if you don't stay in Israel, be the best in your class while you're here, and learn the language – really learn it."

He looked up at me. Softly, he said, "Yeah, okay."

Denis Karalich had little choice but to wait, and he knew it. But that didn't stop his heart from yearning for his family and that was why he wanted to go to Germany, although he would never say it. I recalled the day before. We were driving back from the beach in Tel Aviv. Radoslav sat on the front seat, chatting cheerfully with me. In the mirror I spied Denis, sitting silently in back, staring hard at each car we passed on the freeway. He was looking at families: fathers and mothers and children talking, arguing, laughing, being together, being normal. Suddenly I felt terribly sad, thinking of how deep pain and longing reached down inside him, and I thought, surely there is no pain like that of a child who knows his parents are alive, but does not know, and cannot fathom, all the reasons why he cannot live with them. I said nothing else to Denis then, but made up my mind I had to at least try and help.

On a windy, unseasonably cold morning a few weeks later, I stepped into the registration office for foreigners in the Bavarian city of Augsburg. This was where Denis thought his mother and brother could be found. I presented the name to a bespectacled man behind a desk surrounded by files. In less than a minute he scribbled an address down and a taxi delivered me to an apartment house where no one answered the door. I left a note.

The following morning in a fake-rustic café in the Augsburg train station, I sat with an attractive, nervous blonde woman in her thirties who introduced herself as Magda Karalich, the mother of Denis. She had a radically different story to tell than what I had heard in Sarajevo about her failed marriage. I didn't ask, I didn't press for details. I didn't want to be in a position of judging.

"Do you want to be in contact with your son Denis?" I asked.

She nodded. "Does he want to see me?"

"I honestly don't know. He would never say this to anyone because he's afraid of it not coming true. Denis just says he wants to come to Germany, and I take it there's a reason."

She sat for a minute saying nothing. She searched for words, then started to cry. Softly she said, "Please, do you have any pictures of my Denis?"

I showed her everything I had. She moved them back a bit so her tears wouldn't drop on the prints.

I took a pre-paid telephone card I had just purchased and slid it across the table, along with a scrap of paper with a telephone number on it. Then I went to the phone box and called Mevezerret Ziyyon in Jerusalem and said that Denis Karalich should be waiting at the public telephone later that day. Magda Karalich and I said good-bye, and I left her to call her son.

In the meantime in Sarajevo, Djuro Bozovich's condition had gone from bad to worse. Srdjan Gornjakovich tried to stabilize him, but he needed surgery and not medicine. "He was going to die and he knew it," Srdjan said.

Srdjan and La Benevolencija's medical director Igor Gaon frantically went to work on the two way radio and with the UN. They reached Tuvya Raviv in Budapest, who rang up Tel Hashomer Hospital, home of Israel's premier cardiology unit.

Hanging desperately on to life, Djuro Bozovich made the journey from Sarajevo to Split by UN transport, then on a commercial aircraft to Zagreb. Raviv had a car waiting for him there, which sped him to a hospital in Budapest. By this time his condi-

tion was so precarious doctors doubted he would survive another drive to an airport, much less live through a four hour flight. The problem was, the operation Djuro needed could not be performed in Budapest. Tuvya sent for the car.

* * *

The first exhibition from my Sarajevo work opened in Tel Aviv in June 1994 at Beth Hatefutsoth Museum of the Diaspora. At the opening only two people wore jackets and ties: Radoslav and Denis. By this time they had seen my pictures so often they gave tours to other Sarajevans, who came on a bus rented for them by the Jewish Agency. Looking over the pictures were Natalia and her husband Djuro, who had successfully undergone valve replacement surgery, and had been out of the hospital six weeks. The family had cemented itself back together and Djuro and Natalia were keeping a watchful eye on Denis. Djuro said he didn't think Haris would be leaving Sarajevo any time soon, but that he, Natalia, and Radoslav planned on making Israel their home. "We want to keep Denis with us," he said. "I just wish I had my health and some money. Then I would have taken five children out of Sarajevo." He smiled. "But this one will do."

After the opening night crowd melted away, Gisela Dachs, who wrote a story for Zeit Magazin about the boys and me, took us all to dinner in Tel Aviv. Then Denis and Radoslav and I walked to the Holiday Inn, where they would spend the night, not for the first time, camped out on the floor of my room. Standing on the 9th floor balcony, they ogled at the lights of the city stretching away to the east and just opposite, the waves of the vast, black Mediterranean crashing against the beach. Directly below us were the sidewalk cafés lining Ha' Yarkon Street and the traffic hissing past.

Radoslav went inside to glue himself to the television. Denis and I stayed on the balcony.

"Have you heard from your mother?"

He nodded. "I heard from her once, and my brother called once. They said they'll write soon."

I shuddered inside. It had been eight weeks since I had given her the telephone number and address. "How do you like Israel these days?" I asked.

"Hmm. I'm not sure. I'm best in my class in Hebrew and now I'm starting English. I also play basketball every day and I'm getting good."

109

Denis at school in Jerusalem. April 1994 (above).

Denis and Radoslav at a beach south of Jaffa. April 1994 (below).

"But do you like it here? Is it a place you think you might want to stay?"

"I'm not sure."

Not sure was far better than last time, when he said he wanted to leave Israel as soon as possible. Denis Karalich, now 14 years old, was starting to think with his head, and not only cling to the dreams of a normal family life that lived in his heart.

Just then a motorcycle tore loudly down Ha' Yarkon below us and Denis stretched, in awe, to watch it. "Oh how I'd love to have something like that – or better, a really nice motor scooter."

"Well, the day you start university here, I'll buy you any scooter or motorcycle you want."

"That's in four, maybe five years," he said, as if to caution me.

"Well, that's only if you're still here."

"Well maybe … " Denis Karalich said as he stared out over the lights of Tel Aviv. "Maybe …" But he was smiling.

In the morning the boys went down to the swimming pool, ate pizza on the beach, and then I drove them, sunburned and tired, back home to Jerusalem. Denis fiddled through my cassettes and slipped in the Tom Petty tape just as we turned onto the freeway. He found "Learning to Fly," and cranked up the volume.

While Tom Petty sang, Radoslav, Denis, and I joined loudly, and badly along. I pulled away from the traffic and flew up the mountain toward the Holy City. The boys clapped in rhythm and sang.

"Well some say life will beat you down
Break your heart, steal your crown
So I've started out, for God knows where
I guess I'll know when I get there
I'm learning to fly, but I ain't got wings
Coming down is the hardest thing."

[1]   Written by Tom Petty-Jeff Lynne, copyright 1991 Gone Gator Music / EMI April Music Inc. (ASCAP) All rights reserved. Used by permission.

Denis and Radoslav in Tel Aviv.

113

Afterwards

At the Mevezerret Ziyyon Absorption Center just outside Jerusalem there is a flat with a sign on its door reading "Welcome to Israel." It is the new home of Zeyneba Hardaga and her family, Branumir, Aida, and Stela. They arrived to much fanfare in both the Israeli and international press and were interviewed their first day more times than they could count. Finally they were brought to their new flat and left alone. It was a Friday afternoon.

There was a knock on the door. A television crew from one of the American networks wanted to interview the family. Aida shook her head and told them, "I'm sorry, but it's nearly Shabbat and I know how important this day is in Israel.

Rachela Dzidic in her kitchen in Jerusalem, surounded by her children and their friends.

You'll have to come back on Sunday." Then she closed the door.

Aida intended on settling in Israel for good. "Not many people are granted two lives," she said when I came to see her in April 1994. "God gave us one life. These people gave us another."

She, Branumir, and Stela threw themselves into

learning Hebrew. They studied in school during the day and at home in the evenings. "What's important for me is this – not to say 'thanks.' That's a single word and maybe people use it too often. But because I appreciate what has been done for us, I am going to learn this language, train for work, get a job, and then by being a productive member of this society, I won't have to say 'thanks.' I will show my appreciation by my actions.

"I think it's time we thought about converting to Judaism. After all, Stela should marry a nice Jewish boy, right? And I don't want to put any more barricades in her way than necessary. We have been saved by Israel, we are living in Israel, and we will become Israelis."

A few days later, a car came and collected Zeyneba Hardaga, Branumir, Aida, and Stela. It drove into Jerusalem and up to the doors of the Prime Minister's office. Inside, the family took their place around a conference table. Itzhak Rabin took his place next to Zeyneba Hardaga. Then while the cameras flashed and the video tape rolled, the Prime Minister of Israel handed citizenship papers to the Righteous Gentile from Sarajevo. Zeyneba Hardaga thanked the prime mini-

117

ster for all that had been done for her and her family, for bringing them to Israel, and giving them this new life. The prime minister said "No, Mrs Hardaga, it is we who thank you."

* * *

7:30 am in Mevezerret Ziyyon Absorption Center. The Dzidic household was slowly coming alive. One after the other, Denis and Haris climbed out of bed, hit the bathroom, and donned their school clothes. Rachela woke her husband Atif, and went to make coffee for the grown ups, sandwiches for the boys.

For a moment all was pandemonium as school books and shoes couldn't be found. Friends stopped by to collect the boys for school, who on their way out passed their grandfather Itzhak Levi. Levi said good morning and left a sack of groceries before heading out again. Then in another instant, it turned quiet, peaceful even. Rachela sat down by Atif, poured coffee for the three of us, and began talking.

"It's been only eight weeks now, but I must say things have been easier than I thought they would be. I was so worried about my children, but thank God, they have not changed at all. They are as affectionate as ever and full of personality. And they have found themselves here, chatting away with their friends in Hebrew, going to school, being real Israelis. Haris is back up to his straight A level.

"There have been adjustments, of course. They missed not only their parents, but everything that came with the life we had: their bicycles, toys, computers, clothes. The younger one, Denis, somehow thought that by us reappearing, so would all the things we had in our lives. But they haven't. In Sarajevo, I used to cook up portions of his favorite foods, so when he was hungry he could just go to the freezer, get out what he wanted, and pop it into the microwave. It was almost the first thing he asked for when we arrived, and I laughed and said no, we couldn't do that now. Suddenly he became very quiet, and he said, 'Mom, are we poor?'

"I told him no. We just have to think before we spend our money for a while, and besides, no one has everything they want. I was thinking, of course, about bikes. I said we'd buy them immediately, but Haris and Denis both told us no, they wanted us to have things for the apartment first, and then later we could buy them bikes. I could not have imagined that kind of willing sacrifice in the past, back in our former lives.

"In our absence, you see, Haris was faced with growing up and caring for his little brother. He had to learn to dole out money for him, make sure he washed each morning, and looked over his homework every afternoon. But this was hard for him, although he didn't let on to Denis..

"Now we're a family again. As soon as Atif and I arrived in Israel, we took the children out of school for ten days, and the four of us stayed together constantly. We both took turns sleeping with each of the boys and you can just imagine how much a child has to tell his parents after such a long time.

On the third day we were together, we had a family talk. I have some friends in the United States, and it really wouldn't be so hard for us to move there. We asked the children, and posed the question in terms of the future, and how at home they felt here, as opposed to moving to the US.

"Well Haris turned bright red. He jumped up. 'I don't want to go to America!' he said. 'We won't find a better place than this. We don't want to start all over again in a new country.' Both boys said 'We like it here just fine.' Later that night, after the boys were asleep, Atif and I realized that of all the problems we might have, where to live isn't one of them.

"Sarajevo has changed me, that much I know. I waited too long to leave, I couldn't get out, and I was cut off from my sons. Now that we've lived through all that, nothing we do can be so bad, and I don't believe I can ever make a wrong decision again, not as long as we are together.

"I also know I will never go back to Sarajevo. I knew it even before I left. I knew it in the autumn of 1992. You see, I'll tell you about my friend, Ana Glaban. She was my best friend all through college and we worked together for years. I always thought she was the best mother I knew: patient, loving, and she could never stop talking about her children. Ana lived in Dobrinja, and there was a mortar attack and a shell exploded next door. She heard crying and left her family to run over to help. As soon as she entered the building, another shell exploded and Ana was killed.

"I saw her children at the funeral. It was a Serb funeral and it was a Serb mortar that killed her. She never cared who was Serb or Jew or Muslim or

Zeyneba Hardaga receiving Israeli citizenship from Prime Minister Itzhak Rabin. April 1994

Croat, but there she was in that coffin, and now what's to become of her children? All I could do as I looked at her kids was to think of mine, and how badly I wanted to hold them that day.

"So much of my life is over now. A great deal lies behind me and much of it tragic, some of it horrifying. Something goes out of your life when you cannot walk the streets of your city, the city you were born in and loved so much, especially if you never had the intention of leaving it. And oh, I dearly loved Sarajevo. It pains me to think that I cannot visit my mother's grave. But my father, who lived through so much, has lived to see his family safe, and Atif and I will do whatever we can to make our children feel secure and loved. But when its quiet in the house, and I'm alone, sometimes I'm overcome with sadness. I feel nostalgic for Bosnia, and for Sarajevo."

119

Acknowledgements

There were two principal
underwriters of this project.
At the Doron Foundation for
Education and Welfare I thank
Morechai Mevorach and
Miriam Kaidar and at the
Righteous Persons Foundation
I thank Steven Spielberg.

Not being a war photographer by trade, I would never have thought of going into Sarajevo during the siege if Tom Gjelten of National Public Radio (and author of "Sarajevo Daily") had not constantly harangued me that fall of 1993 with stories of the brave little Bosnian Jewish community. And I probably would not have made that final step had not La Benevolencija's medical director Professor Dr Igor Gaon gone with me by ship from Split to Ancona and on the UNPROFOR cargo plane into Sarajevo itself.

I could not possibly thank all those in Sarajevo who helped me make this book, but many people went to great lengths to see I got the story I wanted. Some risked their lives to do so. If I have produced good photographs and interesting stories, it is only because Sarajevans did everything they could to help me get them. Ivan Ceresnjes and Jacob Finci were the prime movers, Rachela Dzidic did nearly all my translations, and Elias and Ljerka Danon shared their friendship and home with me more than once, even though they had little to share. I also thank the friendly and competent staff of the hotel at the end of the world: the Sarajevo Holiday Inn.

Having worked in this part of the world for several years, there are a few journalist-colleagues whose friendship I treasure, and I thank them for their input while working on this book, especially Chuck Sudetic of the New York Times. I also appreciate the help, advice and wisdom of Alison Smale of Associated Press, Ian Traynor of the Guardian, Anna Maria Tremonti of the Canadian Broadcasting Company, John Kifner of the New York Times, Tom Shanker of the Chicago Tribune and Ruth Gruber.

I am deeply thankful to those newspapers and magazines who worked with me on stories from Bosnia, including: in the US, Ken Ikenberry of the Washington Post, in Germany, Joachim Riedl and Eva Ernst of Süddeutsche Zeitung, Gisela Dachs and Gabriele Vorwerg of Zeit Magazin, and in the Netherlands, Tamara Benima of the Nieuw Israelietisch Weekblad.

I greatly appreciate the support of Bud Levin, Russell Robinson, Amy Stone, Penny Buccafuri, Gerry Nagel, Rabbi Brian Lurie, and Yael Septee at the United Jewish Appeal; Cheryl Mariner and Elie Benson at the Central British Fund for World Jewish Relief; and Ambassador Milton Wolf, Michael Schneider, Amir Shaviv, Miriam Feldman, Yechiel Bar-Chaim, and Jennifer Bodner at the American Jewish Joint Distribution Committee. In the Jewish Agency for Israel's Jerusalem office, Alan Pakes and Shira Ozeri, in Budapest, Tuvya Raviv. Thanks also to Dr Michael Berenbaum of the US Holocaust Memorial Museum, Howard Rieger of the United Jewish Federation of Pittsburgh, David Sarnat of the Atlanta Jewish Federation, and Rabbi Andrew Baker and David Harris of the American Jewish Committee. I also appreciate the support of Charles and Andy Bronfman.

Once again, I thank H. G. von Zydowitz and Nicole Rubbe at *Leica* Cameras, GmbH, for their assistance, advice, and generous support, as well as Henry Froelich of Mamiya Corporation. I am grateful indeed for the kindness extended to me by the Holiday Inn Tel Aviv during the opening of my exhibition and the friendliness the staff showed Denis and Radoslav. All my photographs were printed by Karsten Schirmer in Berlin.

Several museums and galleries helped with exhibitions, some of which were generously supported by the Austrian Cultural Institute. At Beth Hatefutsoth Tel Aviv, I thank Giora Goren, Joel Cahen, Margalith Bergstein and those who arranged everything on remarkably short notice. At the Dorothy McRae Gallery in Atlanta, which premiered this exhibition, I am beholden to director Uri Vaknin. At the Jewish

Historical Museum in Amsterdam, Dr Edward van Voolen, and at the Munich City Museum, Dr Ulrich Pohlmann. Most of all, I thank the Jewish Museum of Vienna: Professor Dr Julius Schoeps, Werner Hanak, and especially Georg Haber for his kindness, understanding, and support.

Dr Christian Brandstätter, whose publishing house in Vienna bears his name, threw himself whole heartedly into this project and designed the book himself. We spent long hours before his layout table in his Vienna atelier, and I marveled as I witnessed one of the last great European book-makers at work. Editor Deborah Wise forged my wayward text and diffuse ideas into a readable story and I appreciate the guidance I received from my German agent Tom Schlück and US agent Sarah Lazin. Thanks also to Katja Erlach and Gabriela Hamböck at Brandstätter.

I close by acknowledging all those whose pictures are in this book. Searching for "the decisive moment," as Henri Cartier Bresson called it, I recorded anguish, pain, tears, and heartbreak. I did this in order to tell the story as best I could. But photography feeds itself on the misery of others, and I am deeply sorry I took some of these pictures and present them to the world at large. I only hope their publication will move readers to help those still in Sarajevo (see following page).

Publication of this book was made possible by the generous support of the following organizations: the American Jewish Joint Distribution Committee, the American Jewish Committee, the Jewish Federation of Atlanta, the Jewish Federation of Cincinnati, the Jewish United Fund of Chicago, the United Jewish Federation of Pittsburgh, the Jewish Community Federation of Greater Rochester, the Combined Jewish Philanthropies of Boston, the Jewish Federation of Houston, the Metrowest Jewish Federation, and at the United Jewish Appeal, the Small Communities, Young Leadership, and Principal Gifts Divisions.

© Radoslav Bozovich

Jevrejsko kulturno-prosvjetno i humanitarno društvo

Jewish cultural-educational and humanitarian society

71000 Sarajevo, Dobrovoljačka 83, POB 331, Tel.071-663-472, 441-735, 652-180, Fax. 663-473

The network of La Benevolencija and its friends stretches across several countries and involves individuals, foundations, and corporations. With an infrastructure of offices, warehouses, and transportation set up by Joint, CBF, and Friends of La Benevolencija in Zagreb and Split, donations have come in many forms. Here are just a few examples: Dr Hiba Trifunovic, in the German city of Osnabruck, sent truckloads of medical supplies and continues to do so. In Italy, Mrs Roberta Orvieto of Rome organized shipments of food. The Union of French Jewish Students mobilized the larger French Jewish community, gathered 76 tons of food, medicine, and clothing, and delivered it to the La Benevoleoncija warehouse in Split. The official Jewish communities of many European states have made contributions, both in cash and goods, CRIF of France, B'nai B'rith in Belgium, The Czech and Bulgarian Jewish communities, the European Council of Jewish Communities, the Jewish community of Vienna.

The European Jewish Congress, provided eight tons of food, and the Soros Foundation has sent 1,300 family packages. Mercedes Benz and Volkswagen corporations provided cash donations and Mediciéns Sans Frontières has provided the bulk of the stock in La Benevolencija's Sarajevo pharmacies. Doctors in Pittsburgh, Pennsylvania shipped 30 cartons of medicine directly to the Split warehouse, Harvard students contributed more than $ 20,000 in cash. Catholic, Orthodox, and Muslim organizations have all helped La Benevolencija help the citizens of Sarajevo.

Those interested in providing aid should contact the following organizations:

What You Can Do To Help

RESCUE
RELIEF
REHABILITATION

In the United States and Canada:
The American Jewish Joint Distribution Committee
711 3rd Avenue
New York, New York 10017
USA
Telephone (001) (212) 687 6200, Fax 370 5467
(donations must be earmarked for La Benevolen-
cija, and can also be made through local Jewish
Federations or the United Jewish Appeal)

In the United Kingdom:
The Central British Fund for World Jewish Relief
Drayton House
30 Gordon Street
London WC1H OAN
Great Britain
Telephone (44) (071) 387 3925, Fax 383 4810

Vrienden van La Benevolencija
Sarajevo
1993

On the European continent:
Friends of La Benevolencija Sarajevo
Keizergracht 104b
NL 1015 Amsterdam
The Netherlands
Telephone (31) (020) 620 4388, Fax 625 4452

"La Benevolencija"
1892
SARAJEVO

La Benevolencija
Zidovska Opcina
Zidovski prolaz 1
58 000 Split
Republic of Croatia
Telephone/Fax (385) (41) 361 420

Captions for the following pages are:

S. 12: Dating from 1571, Il Kal Grande was the first synagogue built in Bosnia by Spanish Jewish refugees. August 1988.

S. 14/15: Keys brought from Spain by the Sephardim. They are now in the Jewish Museum of Bosnia-Hercegovina. January 1994.

S. 20: Zeyneba Hardaga saved Jews during the Second World War and was the first Muslim to receive Israel's Righteous Gentile Award in 1985. November 1993.

S. 23: Ljerka Danon and her war recipe cookbook. December 1993.

S. 26/27: Names of Sarajevans killed during the Second World War, inscribed on the walls of the old Turkish fort of Vraca, above the city. 80 % of the names are Jewish. May 1989.

S. 30: Sarajevans at a memorial service in the former concentration camp in the Croatian city of Djakovo. May 1989.

S. 34: After a foraging trip thorugh Sarajevo to find food, wood and water, a man scurries across a street exposed to snipers. January 1994.

S. 38: Sarajevo university library. May 1989.

S. 39: Sarajevo university library. November 1993.

S. 48: La Benevolencija, the Sarajevo Jewish community's humanitarian aid agency, has 54 volunteers, of whom only 24 are Jewish. The rest are Serbs, Muslims, and, like 20 year old Vlado, Croats. November 1994.

S. 56: A dentist visited the Jewish community twice each month during the siege. January 1994.

S. 60/61: Titzko, the community cook, uses three stoves: one for electricity, another for gas, a third for wood. December 1993.

S. 68/69: Dr and Mrs Wagman at home. Mrs Wagman is lighting her wood burning stove, which she uses for heat and cooking. January 1994.

S. 72: The Jewish community medical staff has made over 650 house calls during the siege, many of them by Srdjan Gornjakovich, a 31 year old Serb physician. December 1993.

S. 82: Jews bringing their belongings to the synagogue, in advance of their leaving Sarajevo on the JDC rescue convoy of February 1994.

S. 86/87: Community leaders checking the convoy list. January 1994.

S. 98: Denis Karalich, left, and Radoslav Bozovich, are the Jewish community's water boys, and best of friends. November 1993.

S. 103: Denis in the Sarajevo Jewish community center. November 1993.

S. 104/105: Haris Karalich bids goodbye to his son Denis, about to leave Sarajevo on the Jewish community convoy. February 1994.

S. 111: Radoslav batting his Gameboy. April 1994.

S. 114/115: Wearing t-shirts displaying their names in Hebrew, Radoslav and Denis visit the Western Wall in Jerusalem's Old City.